M. C. Johnston

Mar. 1947.

AN AMERICAN YEAR

MISSOURI WHEAT FARMERS BY JOE JONES

AN AMERICAN YEAR

COUNTRY LIFE AND
LANDSCAPES THROUGH THE SEASONS
BY *Hal Borland* WITH ILLUSTRATIONS
BY DISTINGUISHED CONTEMPORARY
ARTISTS

Simon and Schuster, New York

FOR DON AND HAL JR.

SOME OF THE ESSAYS IN THIS BOOK APPEARED FIRST ON
THE EDITORIAL PAGES OF THE NEW YORK TIMES. MY
THANKS TO THE TIMES AND TO ITS EDITOR, MR. CHARLES
MERZ, FOR PERMISSION TO USE THAT MATERIAL AS I
HAVE USED IT HERE. — H.B.

Contents and List of Illustrations

EVENING IN MARCH BY JACKSON LEE NESBITT

MARCH. SPRING EQUINOX. An

equinox is a matter of celestial mechanics, but Spring is a tide that rises in the human heart. Not in the heart alone, to be sure, for it is an earth tide which is transmitted to the human pulse by some subtle osmosis; but there is where it beats upon our senses, there is where it strikes the quick.

It is more than change. Change comes day by day and even hour by hour; change is a law of life. It is more than a warm rain or a sun overhead, more even than a leaf thrusting up through the mold of the past. It is an understanding of all these things and a realization that today is but a part of all the yesterdays and all the tomorrows that have walked across this earth.

A swamp maple shows moistly black where the rising sap oozes from a gash made during the Winter's clearing. I touch a finger to the ooze and test it with my tongue, and I am tasting last Summer's sunlight and next Summer's shade. A flock of early blackbirds gabbles in the marsh reeds, and I am hearing the winds of Carolina in December, the drone of June bees over a Connecticut clover field.

Somewhere up there the stars and planets wheel into line, and we have another equinox. And down here the earth quivers imperceptibly, a root wedges its way between two grains of sand, a bird sings. And the pulse in the human heart quickens for a brief moment, knowing that another Spring is at hand.

T H E grackles are here, and setting up such a clamor one can scarcely think. They have been here several days, but until this morning they hadn't settled in my woods; now it sounds as though someone out there were pouring shelled corn into a gigantic steel tank. I undertook to count them, but the best I could do was count those in one tree and draw an estimate from that. There were seventy-eight in one oak and they filled twenty-six trees. And the ground beneath the trees was black with them, a dark, maggoty mass of movement. There must be at least five thousand in this one congregation.

Even inside the house we must shout to make ourselves heard above their clamor. And when they take wing it is with a roar as from a waterfall or a flight of planes close overhead. Worst of all, they come and go, fretfully, uncertainly, and always with that gabbling, dry-corn clatter while they are perched or on the ground.

If the grackle were only a beautiful bird—or if it had a sweet voice—such a mass visitation would be a delight. But I can see no beauty in the bird this morning except the bronze sheen on its dark feathers. Perhaps its screeching voice and abominable social habits prejudice me; it is forever squabbling and has all the outward signs of a trouble-seeker, even among its own kind.

I refuse to be impressed by sheer numbers or by a glitter of bronze light on a feather. Most of all, I refuse to be silenced by a chorus of creaking gate hinges, no matter what the ornithologists may call them. And I am in a mood to demand why I should respect any ornithologist who classifies a grackle as a songbird.

MAN is not an aquatic animal, but from the time we stand in youthful wonder beside a Spring brook until we sit in old age and watch the endless roll of the sea we feel a strong kinship with the waters of this world. We marvel at the magnificence of a snowflake, a water crystal.

An American Year

THE ROBERT E. LEE AND THE NATCHEZ BY JOHN MC CRADY

We sleep content with the drone of rain on the roof. We slake our thirst with the cool waters of the earth. And we go forth at this time of year to see and hear the little streams trickling down all the hills of Spring.

It was such little streams, grown big with April warmth, that carved our valleys. The silt they carried down from the hilltops enriched the meadows and built delta lands. Grass followed in their wake, and trees. And when men first traveled they followed such streams, first along their banks and then upon their swirling currents. They followed flowing waters to the ocean, and in due time put forth upon the ocean itself. Their towns were river towns, and their first cities faced the sea.

6

The trickling waters are awake now and creeping through the grass roots, down the late March hillsides. The swamps ooze with their slow drainage and ponds brim over at the edge. Streams test their banks. Floods are in the making. The very earth seems sodden underfoot. And if we reach back far enough in the racial memory we must know that we are seeing the ooze and flow, not of one early Spring alone but of the very Springtime of the earth, when the land and life itself rose out of the waters of long ago.

WE have been disputing the way with bull briar, clearing it from the paths and out of the underbrush; and a painful, tedious job it is. The green stems are not only tough; they are armed with thorns that can give one's hand a nasty gash. And they climb like a wild grape. One needs a machete to deal with them properly, and heavy gloves to haul the severed stems out of the trees.

We call them bull briars or cat briars, but the botanists know them as one of the smilaxes. And William Bartram was a good enough botanist to forget their thorns and extol their dubious virtues. In the South he found that the Seminoles dug their knotty roots, chopped them up, mashed them in a mortar, and strained off a mushy sediment which dried into a fine, reddish meal. They mixed this meal with water and honey and made what Bartram describes as "a beautiful, delicious jelly, very nourishing and wholesome." He also reports that they sometimes mixed this meal with fine corn flour to make a batter which they fried in bear grease, and he likens this product to fritters.

If there are any Seminoles within hearing, I should like them to know that I have quite a patch of bull briar—or contee, as they called it—ready for the digging. They can have every root on my place, and I won't even ask for a taste of that "beautiful, delicious jelly" which they can make from it. All I require is that they take the stems with the roots, for when they have been cut and left to dry in the underbrush they are like a snarl of barbed wire. I know, for I extricated myself from such a snarl not an hour ago.

A PAIR of bluebirds has been flirting through the woods, now that the grackle hordes have moved on. The grackles simply picked up and went, for no obvious reason. They couldn't have exhausted the food supply of these acres; the insects are still emerging from the soft earth in myriads. Probably some old hen grackle got restless and the others followed, for they appear to be as full of mob instincts as human beings. Anyway, they are gone and the bluebirds are here.

Their blue is startlingly brilliant, the blue of a western sky, and the red of their breasts is the color of a July sunburn on a blond skin. And they are quiet. They sing, a pleasantly musical little song; after the grackle clamor it is like the soft tinkle of an old-fashioned music box. They are welcome to stay as long as they like.

Maeterlinck spoiled my pleasure in bluebirds for a long time. Until I read his play, the bluebird was a beautiful bit of avian life which belonged to the Spring woods. Its habits were exemplary and both its plumage and its song were delightful. But Maeterlinck, by symbolizing the bluebird and making its pursuit the be-all and end-all of life, ruffled my perverse reactions. It was as though a critical maiden aunt had held

8

up to me, as an imperative example, a simpering little goody-goody boy who never scuffed his shoes or had a dirty face. If I ever had liked the little paragon, I would now despise him.

But the bluebird and I have now lived down Mr. Maeterlinck's play. I know the bluebird also has tantrums and peccadillos and there is a place in my heart, and my woods, for it. Particularly in late March, just after a visitation from the grackles.

BRINGING IN THE SAP BY PHILIP CHENEY

APRIL.

IN THIS latitude one never really knows whether April is Spring or not. Red maple buds are ready to open and may burst tomorrow or wait another two or three weeks. Willows could put out leaves this week, but daren't venture yet. To be sure, day lilies are well up and tulips are getting ready to unfurl their shoots into leaves. Crocuses have opened, hesitantly, in more favored places. Lilacs have fat buds waiting for a warmer sun. Spice bush and nannyberry have completed their March preparations and are ready to respond to April encouragement—if and when it comes. But they, and others, can wait another two weeks, and they may wait that long, if April has its usual tantrums.

An American Year

That's the thing about April: it has tantrums. It is by turns a backward child among the months and a mischievous youngster with disarming wisdom and consideration. It will bring frost and cold rain and even snow flurries; and it will bring days that belong to late May—warm mornings, hot afternoons and balmy nights. It will get you out in the garden in your shirt sleeves in the morning and have you shivering before a hearth fire the same evening. It will flatter you off guard, then kick you in the shins.

A part of it is our own impatience to see Spring move in with flowers in her hair. We're weary of waiting. But the greater part of it is simply April being April. We know what's coming and we'll welcome it, but we still don't like the way that April brings it. April's a problem child.

S O M E H O W the belief has got around that life in the country is something like a perpetual vacation. Probably country folk themselves are to blame, because so many of them put on their best bib and tucker when visitors arrive from the city and devote the whole week end to enjoying life. And the visitors go away firm in the belief that once they acquire a few acres of their own they can live that kind of week-end life every day in the year.

That isn't true, of course. But even country folk who write about their own lives often help perpetuate the illusion. On paper, at least, they are enjoying life, and they say so, forgetting to dwell on the sweat that goes into stony or sterile fields before the succulent crops come out, the drudgery that goes into the preserving kettle before the jars are filled, the backbreaking labor needed to build a stone wall or convert a smokehouse into quaint guest quarters with chintz curtains. In ignoring these matters they aren't necessarily trying to sell anybody a bill of goods. They are only

12

insisting that they enjoy life, work and all, and implying that they take the work in stride, which they often do.

But make no mistake about it, life in the country is not all loafing in the sun or going fishing or eating strawberry preserves. It's cutting firewood and shoveling snow and weeding the garden and hoeing corn and thawing out the pump, too. Ask any seven-days-a-week farmer. Or ask me, tonight. I'm no farmer. I spent a novitiate at that job, then worked for many years in various cities before I came back to the land to live. I'm no farmer now; I'm simply a countryman. But I've spent the past week, almost every daylight hour of it, laying up a stone wall, and I'm in a mood to give an eloquent answer to such a question.

IT was a raw, murky morning with snow clouds hiding the sunrise, April in dismal dress. We sat at breakfast facing the lower acre, which will be full of cranesbill and jack-in-the-pulpits in another month; but from where we sat beside the big dining room window it was a drab patch of soggy woodland with only a brush pile to catch the eye, a pile we were going to burn next week.

I was watching for the first snowflakes when she appeared, a thin-flanked mother cottontail. She was there, sitting on a clump of trout lily mat, before I saw any movement. Then four youngsters were beside her, gray little puffballs with ears no longer than the first joint on my little finger. They began to nurse, and the mother was all attention, ears cupped, head swiveling as she watched for danger.

The youngsters sucked as eagerly as pups, waggling their nubbin-tails, nudging each other aside. One lost his grip on a dug and rolled down the clump and shook himself and clambered back. One butted the mother, as a calf would. One rolled half over, still holding the dug and

13

wriggling in ecstasy, and the mother pushed him aside with a front paw. Then two of them sat back, apparently full for the moment, and rubbed their faces, catlike; and the mother put an end to the meal by hopping away a few steps. And there they were, all four of those babies—I could have hidden any one of them in my palm—shaking their ears, rubbing their milky muzzles.

The mother gave some signal neither visible nor audible to us and two of them scurried into the brush pile. A third vanished behind it. The fourth, the inevitable individualist, remained in solitary daring for fully a minute. Then his audacity overwhelmed him and he, too, plunged into the brush pile.

I decided the brush could stay there a while longer.

A MONTH ago the silence of Winter was thick on the evening air. The nights had the quiet of starlight and the days had a frosty reticence, for Spring had not yet stirred.

Go out of doors now, at dusk, at sunup or at noon, and you can hear the change. It's a welcome sound, particularly when the weather turns perverse; a reassuring sound that has the constant turn of the year in its faintest echo. In the dusk, the peepers, the cricket frogs; in the morning, the robins, the song sparrows and their cousins; before noon, the cardinals and the blackbirds and the woodpeckers—these are the obvious voices, those that can be heard above the ordinary sounds of the open countryside.

But one must listen closely for the lesser voices. Sit on a stone wall beside an open woodland or in a meadow or an old orchard, and relax the pores of understanding. Because the ear is none too keen in April, you seem to feel rather than hear them. The ants, already hurrying; a

SPRINGTIME BY JOHN E. COSTIGAN

few bees, bewildered but seeking their slim rations; an occasional stiff-legged beetle—the rangers and foragers of an insect army.

A warm rain or two, a bit more sun, and the whisper will become a murmur, then a chorus. For there is movement underfoot, a vast swelling, seething, strengthening upthrust of life. The egg hatches, the seed sprouts, the bud opens. There is no stopping the earth in its rounds, the

15

seasons in their turn, the simple reaching of a grass-blade toward the sun. There will be no more silence until another harvest time has passed.

THE day's work done, the supper eaten, the countryman smokes a slow pipe over his newspaper, pausing often to stare unseeing at a page. At last he gets pen and paper and goes into the dining room, settles down at the big table where he has room for thoughts as well as elbows.

"Dear Son," he writes, "I was plowing today and noticing how good the soil smells. Just the way it smelled thirty years ago when I first set a plow to this farm. It's the smell of Spring, I guess. The willows down along the stream are not in leaf yet, for it's a late Spring, but you can see the green in their buds. A couple of boys were down there fishing today, the way you used to. Never were many fish there, but it's fishing that matters, this time of year, not fish.

"Spring is late, as I said. Your mother's early daffodils are in bloom, but the lilacs aren't in full leaf yet. If you were here you would be fretting, anxious to hurry things along. But the more Springs I see, the more I realize there's some things you can't hurry. And Spring always comes."

Spring—Winter's end and new growth's beginning. Like sunrise, in a way, and the start of a new day. . . . He finishes the letter and seals and stamps it, and he opens the side door and stands there a full minute, watching the stars and feeling the night wind and sensing his world, his Spring-palpitant world, before going to bed.

THE peepers came out early, tuning up for Spring's first full moon. Then came the snowstorm, which not only silenced the peepers but gave the fox sparrows and robins and blackbirds a few miserable days. One flock of birds, however, seemed to know what was coming. Six hours ahead of the snow a wedge of Canada geese came winging up the valley,

THE POND IN THE HILLS BY HANS KLEIBER

apparently just in from the South, swung northwest across the hills—so low that a person on the ground could see their white neckerchiefs—and kept right on going.

The geese and the peepers didn't belong together, and if the little frogs with the big voices heard the clear whistling of the gray wings they hurried back to their shelters. They were quiet that evening, at any rate. But the songbirds were caught right out in the open. They had been coming into and through this district in what seemed considerably larger numbers than usual for the past couple of weeks.

17

An American Year

But soon after the snow had ceased falling the robins were down in the underbrush shoveling snow to get at the dead leaves and what might be under them. So were the ruddy-backed fox sparrows, which can scratch for a living with the best Leghorn hen. The peepers, however, were quiet, and the geese were probably far away.

Who ever said "silly as a goose" anyway? Robins and peepers may think they know Spring when they see it, but a Canada goose doesn't stand on ceremony, seasonal or otherwise, when a snowstorm is fanning his tail feathers.

IN THE drizzling rain we cleaned the wood ashes from the big fireplace today. Cleaned is perhaps too absolute a word, for at least two reasons: first, we took out only about half the Winter's accumulation, though there were six pailfuls; second, it is not a clean operation, from any housewife's point of view, for the fine ash inevitably sifts about the room and demands a dusting when the ash removers have gone their masculine way.

The fireplace looks empty and I am not sure the fire will burn properly without its ample bed. But this is the time to put the ashes where they will do the most good, for now their salts will leach into the soil and be absorbed by hungry roots before the seeping waters can carry them away. We feed the roses with them and we dig them into the flower beds, thus restoring some of the potash we let wither in the flower vases last Summer. It is our homage to growth and color, the best we can do just now. Perhaps some of the flame that sprang from those ashes through the Winter months will light up the garden in the weeks ahead, and thus we may enjoy our hearth fire twice over.

Grandmother treasured her wood ashes, not for the garden but for the soap kettle. She used them in the Fall, at butchering time, adding them to the fat and simmering the mixture until it had become back-country soap. Lye did the job more quickly, but she had the notion, and probably she was right, that soap made with wood ashes was a milder soap. In her girlhood they used wood ashes, too, in the making of hominy. But that is too slow a process for most hominy makers of today. Indeed, does anyone still make hominy at home?

THERE'S no use trying to keep it quiet any longer. For a while there was hope that each new day might make it possible to forget the whole thing; but these matters are so easily exaggerated that rumors are bound to get started.

The fact is that those radishes planted two weeks ago sprouted and came up wearing topcoats. Rather hastily tailored, but topcoats just the same. Some say that they had wool socks, too; but investigation doesn't bear that out. It might as well be labeled as the unfounded rumor that it is.

I hear, moreover, that just down the road there are carrot seedlings whose first leaves are green only at midday. Mornings they are a livid, goose-pimply red; late afternoons they turn white—somebody called it a scared-out-of-their-wits white, but I don't believe that; it, too, savors of alarmist rumor.

At the upper end of our garden a row of early peas showed one set of exploratory leaves last Wednesday. When first seen, they were quivering as from an ungovernable chill, but there probably was a light breeze blowing at the time. I investigated the next morning, however, and found that although the whole row had sprouted the leaves had risen only to within half an inch of the surface and then turned back and

19

headed downward. It could be that they were seeking warmth, but I suspect that the boy who planted them merely put the seed in upside down.

These matters are set forth only for the record, but they may serve a nobler purpose. There's nothing like the truth to put an end to irresponsible rumor.

BOTANISTS call them *erythronium,* but country folk know them as dogtooth violets, spotted adder's-tongues, or trout lilies. Whatever the name, they will soon be doing April justice in the moist woodland, their butter-yellow blossoms reaching on long stems toward the midday sun. Their purple-splotched leaves are now thick as hair on a dog's back in the spicebush lowlands.

If they are late in coming it will be the sun's fault, for these miniature yellow lilies are as sensitive as morning-glories to murky days. But a few days of clear skies bring their leaves shooting from the ground in mid-April. Almost as soon as the leaves are fully out the flower stalk appears. Another burst of sun and there they are, all six petals curled back and the stamen heads brown with pollen open to early insects. Queen bumblebees seek them out particularly and small white and yellow butterflies which seem strangely out of place in April.

In the woods they are lovely. Come upon a patch of them unexpectedly and it is like finding the Milky Way strewn out at your feet. But they lose half their beauty once they are picked and taken indoors. They try to respond, but they are flowers of the woods and open skies.

Youngsters used to roam the fields in late April seeking flowers for May baskets, and though many a dogtooth violet went into the bouquets they seldom lasted out the day. They belong to those moist thickets where another month will see the Summer's shade already closing in. April is their month, while the sun can still reach them with its Spring summons.

WE have been quarrying rocks from the vegetable garden most of the day, and now I know why the sons of the first colonists along this northeastern shore of America moved west. America expanded simply because the farmers grew weary of fighting the rocks in this soil. Go over the Alleghenies into the Great Valley and you wonder why farming folk sat so long on this seaboard.

Rocks and stumps, I am convinced, had as much to do with our expansion as the ambitions of statesmen and politicians or the wanderings of trappers and traders. That, to be sure, oversimplifies the matter; but I can still hear my grandmother tell how her father left the cut-over land of eastern Ohio and kept going west until he found the stone-free, stumpless land of Nebraska, and how he gloried in it. And I know, too, how migrants from the rocky hills of New England blossomed and expanded in speech and character when they reached a Midwest where their plows could cut a clean, deep furrow.

My rocks, of course, are migrants themselves. The ice brought them here perhaps twenty-five thousand years ago. When I grub them from the soil—what an understatement that is: grub!—I am pitting my strength and my determination against the forces that shaped this land itself. But man is a stubborn brute, and I will grow tomatoes and carrots here beneath this ancient ice sheet if it drains the last drop of sweat from my aching body. I, too, am an elemental force shaping this land. I am digging a vast pit in which to plant a tomato.

21

An American Year

PLANTING BY THOMAS HART BENTON

F O R those who would look, the woodlands now have a prime display of what specialists in the industrial field would call packaging. Buds are opening, and if any professional packer ever stowed away half as much into as small a space as the trees and bushes reveal in their buds he could rightly cry triumph supreme.

Look at the beeches and you will find each stem tipped with a lance point not much larger than a pencil lead; the green already showing there, as the scales fall away, will become a leaf half as big as a human hand. On the twigs of the gray birches which have been bowing under every heavy rain are buds not a quarter of an inch long; peel away the scales and you can unfurl from them at least two and sometimes five perfect birch leaves, every vein in sight, but still so small that not even a flea could hide under them.

On the dogwood, buds are fattening that have been there all Winter long. Now they are about the size and shape of a praying mantis' head. Open one with care and you will find within it the marvelously folded cream-white leaves which will enfold the flower when it blossoms, four broad leaves in a packet the size of an insect's head. And on the grapeleaf viburnum there are clustered flower buds like pinhead beads with tightly furled leaves enclosing them like two cupped hands.

But for the master display of all, find a shagbark hickory and be patient. One warm day its buds will have grown to the size of a finger. Then they will have forced back their green husks and revealed a fine pink capsule the size of a small thumb. The sun will beam and the pink sheath will open, and out will come not one leaf but five, or even seven, unfurling even while you watch the miracle.

THE Carboniferous age, time when the great coal beds were laid down in the form of tree ferns, has thrust its anachronistic head up along my roadside. Spore heads of the horsetails, which the botanists call *equise-tum,* have appeared overnight, flesh-pink thumbs that look, at a glance, like some unfamiliar fungus. Examine them more closely and you see that there is a firm, succulent stem banded at regular intervals with leaf-like bracts and ending in a head of regularly sworled blossomlike spore

23

cases. The first comparison that comes to mind is the bud head of a mullein. But these are not true blossoms; they are cups in which the spores are brought to maturity.

These spore spikes from another age are stiff and brash and sand-papery to the touch; and rightly so, for they are rich in silica, of which sand itself is made. They will stand thus for perhaps a week, browning a bit more each day as the spores mature. Then the spores will be gone, scattered to the wind, and the shoots will relax as though all the silica and inner strength had been drained out. But alongside will be fresh young shoots of green, the horsetails themselves rising from the rootstock which sent the spore heads up into the light to get their job over with early.

These green shoots belong to that group of plants sometimes called scouring rushes, for they all have that brash, sandy feel. Along the road they will grow into a bushy, knee-high hedge; and if I should take a sickle to them it would sing as though it were cutting spun glass. And each time I pass I shall be tempted to get down on my knees and peer into the miniature jungle, half expecting to be charged by a miniature dinosaur.

T H E way to plant a garden is on your knees. You have to bow to the earth. You must get your fingers in the soil—bare fingers that can feel the inner warmth of Spring. Now and then you will pause and sit back on your heels and listen to the cardinal whistling in the maples that stand in opening bud against the April sky. When you return to the task the sun will be hot on the back of your neck; you may even shed a few drops of sweat into the open seed drills.

You know this soil. You know the feel of it, the smell, the growing warmth within it. You have spaded it, raked it, removed the stones, put in the fertilizer. You feel it here beneath your knees, firm and enduring. It has been here for untold ages, and it was green with life long before man came to stir it for his own purposes or even to press a hurrying footstep into it. You know it for your own because it has welcomed you each Spring that you have come to commune with it.

It will be here for ages after you have gone, each season's moldering leaves adding to it, each Spring's return clothing it once more with green. Seeds will fall here, and take root, and come to flower and fruit. Leaves will cover it in Autumn, and Winter frost will heave and leaven it for Spring and growth.

Kneeling here in the sun, you know these things. Understanding creeps up and through you out of the earth itself. And you cover the seed and mark the row, and move on to the next.

AGAINST THE WIND BY W. R. LOCKE

MAY.

MAY'S COMING. May, with a bouquet of apple blossoms in one hand, a rainbow in the other, bees buzzing round her head and sunlight in her hair. And, we hope, bringing a few week ends when a gardener can leave his rubber boots behind when he goes out to take a look at things.

May's coming, and high time it is. Violets are prepared and eager to make the lowlands purple with blossom. Tulips are reaching toward the shrouded sun. Dogwood buds are fat and anxious. Shadbush could be persuaded into bloom with only a few warm days. And Canada mayflowers—some call them false lilies of the valley—are ready to greet the new month with a flood of fragrance in the upland woods.

Lilacs are late, as is almost everything green this year; but they need only a little encouragement. Grape hyacinths did their best, but a good many of them simply gave up in April and are waiting for May to open wide. Early daffodils struggled through, but there's still a generous garland of them for May's coming. And there will soon be forget-me-nots and dwarf iris in the garden, cranesbill, moccasin flower, and jack-in-the-pulpit in the open. Early peas are scarcely tall enough to tempt a hungry rabbit, and the first planting of lettuce was drowned out. But I'm not complaining; I'm rejoicing. May's coming!

EVERY garden should have a tree nearby. A tall tree with broad bole and spreading branches, preferably branches that start well down the trunk or a low crotch from which a boy might climb. A tree that spreads its roots where it springs from the earth, firm-based and strong against the storms.

This is a tree for man as well as boy, the man who has climbed his trees and now can sit beneath them in understanding. For him, those branches offer shade and hospitality when the sun has seared his neck and the garden is only half weeded. He can rest his back against that broad bole in Spring, when the spading is half done. Weeding and spading that younger hands once hastened through.

There is reassurance at the foot of such a tree, as well as rest. The years have added to its strength and stature. The wind, the rain, the ice and the blistering sun have all gone into the toughness of its fiber. Its roots strike deep into the soil and find sustenance in the old, old hills.

Youngsters must climb trees, to look out across a world that is misty with adventure. New horizons can be seen from tall trees when one is young. But the time comes when one can sit at the foot of such a tree and

THE PATRIARCH BY W. R. LOCKE

see even farther than the eye could reach from its highest branch. For by then the eyes are spanning years instead of miles; by then one can see horizons of love and understanding.

THE hairy woodpeckers seem to be more numerous this Spring than usual; perhaps it is only that we see more of them, for they have grown accustomed to us through a Winter's visits to the feeding station. My one criticism is that they are too quiet. Their call is bright and almost lilting,

29

but I seldom hear it; more often I hear the thinner call of the little downy woodpecker which is, as Grandmother would say, a piert bird, though it has no scarlet crown.

I shall never cease to marvel at the way a hairy works around a branch, head cocked as though listening for the wiggle of a worm; and how he strikes his quarry every time he drives his chisel beak into the wood. If he makes a false move, I have never caught him at it. Not on a tree.

I did catch one in a mistake last Winter, but the error only proved his ingenuity. A Summer visitor had tacked a suet box on a tree, but other birds had eaten away the suet until there was only a big marble of it, too far from the retaining screen for this woodpecker to reach. He surveyed the problem, then settled down on one end of the box and chipped a hole. But his calculations were wrong; he still could not reach that suet. He returned to the front and reappraised the situation. Then he went to the back, where the box overlapped the curve of the tree, and cut a second hole. This time he was precisely right. He got the suet ball.

So I respect the hairy woodpecker for his intelligence, for such it certainly is. But I have my doubts about some of his cousins. About the red-headed woodpecker, for instance, which spent a whole Summer blunting his beak on the corrugated iron roof of a wagon shed.

EVEN the dictionary recognizes Spring Fever for approximately what it is. Only approximately, however. To call it a "lazy, listless feeling" is to underrate it and to ignore completely its deeper manifestations. And to say that it simply comes with "the first warm days of Spring" is to pay only the slightest attention to its real causes.

One can rise to the heights of Spring Fever only briefly. Rise? Of course! One lifts his soul and spirit after a long Winter's drudging effort, and rises to a momentary height where everyday affairs—work in particular—are of utterly no consequence. Thought and action are put in their proper place and sheer feeling takes command. One briefly senses the sole importance of the enduring verities—the sun's warmth, the earth's pulse, the bird on the bough and the blossom on the twig. One is suspended in time with them. Nothing else matters, unless it is sleep. Sleep, and a grassy bank caressing one's shoulder blades. A whole Winter's lost sleep must be compressed into a few brief days of Spring Fever.

Then it's over. The letdown comes—recovery, some call it, having no imagination or sense of proportion. One sinks back into routine, where it is important to work, to worry, to live according to the dictates of the clock. But it's wonderful while it lasts. It's the nearest return to boyhood that is left in the adult world.

T H E radish is an insidious vegetable. It has raised more false hopes and heartburn in the breasts of aspiring gardeners than all the adjectives in the overenthusiastic pamphlets and catalogues. The emotional bite of the radish is equalled only by the sensory bite of its irascible cousin, the horse-radish.

Anyone can grow radishes, more's the pity. Scratch a footpath, drop a few seeds, and two days later radish leaves are reaching for the sun. They neither tire nor discourage. Aphids ignore them, cutworms will have none of them, bugs and beetles that fatten on the veriest weeds pass them by. Certain maggots will attack them in extremity, but only in what must be dire extremity. So the novice at planting looks at his radish crop and says, "Why all the to-do about gardening? There's nothing to it! Behold!"

Then he looks at his lettuce, his beans, his carrots and peas and tomatoes. And whether or not he has eaten his radishes, the heartburn begins. Not even an onion will grow as a radish. Not even a turnip. Why, even spinach will fold its leaves like the Arabs and silently pine away alongside the flourishing radish. Radishes grow. The rest of the garden has to be grown.

True, the radish is pretty to look upon, all bright and shiny red or icy white in fresh-washed splendor. And it has a sweet crispness between the teeth. It is uninhibited by vitamins and uninhabited by any nourishment worth noting. It has the fresh, clean taste of Spring. But that just about exhausts its virtues. And the fact remains that a pair of radish leaves—a whole row of them, for that matter—doesn't make either a garden or a gardener.

IT rained last night, and well do I know it. I had gone to the city to attend a meeting which lapped far over into the evening and, being a countryman, I missed my train. The next was a local which did not leave until midnight and did not get me to my station until 1:15 A.M. Those at home had given me up, thinking I would stay in the city, so I must walk if I would get to my own bed.

The stars were gone and since mine is a rural district there were no lights along the road. But my eyes soon accustomed themselves to the darkness and I could see from quite a distance the massive shape of the old giant of a sycamore which stands where the country road cuts off from the main highway. But before I reached the bank where the myrtle grows in a magnificent carpet the darkness was riven by a flame of lightning. By its light I saw a wondrous mass of clouds racing across the sky. Then the thunder began to roll between the hills, there was more lightning, and I heard the rush that I knew was rain.

There was no escaping it. I was still nearly a mile from home. But

ROAD TO PROVINCETOWN BY JULIAN LEVI

I have found that after the first dousing one can enjoy a rain in any clothes. This one came in torrents, and within fifty yards my shoes were full and squushing. There was no use hurrying since I was already drenched, so I took my time, pausing to listen to the rattle of the drops on the new leaves of the maples. It is a pleasant sound, quite different from the swish of rain through the birches with their limber heads and loose stems. And there was an eerie light in the streams that were soon rushing down the roadside—light from some source I could not discover, for the stars were blanketed.

33

An American Year

So I climbed my hill, squudging along with no companions but wind and rain and the rattle of wet leaves and the rush of unseen streams. And the sweetness of rain was in my nostrils, and the earth tang that rises from the woodlands newly drenched.

It was still raining when I found my bed, and I went to sleep to the farmer's favorite Spring music, the steady trickle of rain from the eaves.

AN apple orchard is a magnificent sight in early May, breath-taking in its expanse of blossom and awesome in its symmetry. Downwind, you can catch its fragrance half a mile away. When you see a whole orchard in full bloom against a hillside, you think that nothing can excel it. But there is one thing that can, for me, at least—a lone apple tree living in abandonment at the edge of a meadow.

It is gnarled, this tree. It is twisted and one-sided. There's an open hollow where once there was a sturdy fork, the mark of a sleet storm that brought a huge branch crashing down years ago. Its remaining limbs are an unchecked tangle of shoots that ran out of encouragement before they got where they started out for. But the whole living side of it is now tufted with bloom. Not a cloud of bloom; clusters of it, like cloud puffs in a Summer sky. And its fragrance comes in wisps rather than a flood.

An orchardist would laugh at the old tree. A woodcutter would scarcely give it a second look. Even small boys will pass up the few knotty apples it will eventually achieve. And next Winter another sleet storm may bring it down completely. But just now it is magnificent. Across the way is a whole orchard, lovely in the lavish finery of a debutante. But here stands an old lady full of years who can still manage a few choice blossoms in her hair.

34

BROWN thrashers are back in our woods again, acting as though they owned them, and towhees are flitting through the underbrush and scratching in the leaves. It's May, all right, and the chorus of warblers is beginning. Some of them are already swooping past the casual observer, and there must be many more that are not so bold, for the mornings are full of song.

The distinguishing mark of the accomplished ornithologist, to most of us, is that he can identify, either by sight or sound, more than half a dozen warblers. There are said to be more than one hundred and fifty species and subspecies of warblers here in America. Most of them sing beautifully—and most of them appear yellow and black in some combination. They flash into sight, spill a little song and are gone, and even though I have pored over the color charts I blink and say, "Maybe it was a bluewing. Or were its wings blue? Maybe it was a Brewster. Was its throat all yellow? Or a Lawrence, perhaps. Did it have a black-throat patch?"

Of course, there are also cerulean warblers and black-throated blue warblers and black and white warblers. But which is which at a glance, among them?

Probably that's why I like the catbird, impertinent as he is, and the insolent blue jay and the industrious robin. There's no mistaking them; they're old friends. And so are the thrashers and towhees, though they are less tolerant of human company. I like to hear the warblers, but I can't get really familiar with a bird that I can identify only with a full-color chart, a pair of field glasses and, to make sure, the company of an ornithologist.

JACK-IN-THE-PULPIT stands tall in the moist lowlands, its twin three-lobed leaves almost tropical and its purple-striped spathe with the

35

hood flapped over, making one think of some little grandmother with a shawl around her shoulders and one corner up over her head.

Botanically, it is an arum, cousin to both the lovely calla lily and the rank-smelling skunk cabbage. Strictly speaking, its flowers are hidden deep within the spathe or sheath—the "pulpit" of our imagination. They neither need nor like the sun, these flowers. Small insects, gnats in particular, seek them out, wallow in the grayish-purple pollen and complete the fertilization. And in the Autumn, when the leaves have withered away and the sheath is no more than a papery husk, the stalk stands in the slanting sun with a fat cluster of lacquer-red berries.

Indians knew it as a food plant, the Senecas in particular digging its fat, round root, drying it and roasting it to make a kind of pasty bread. Thence came the name "Indian turnip." But unless that root is well dried and amply roasted it has a fiery bite for the tongue; it is, on reliable authority, poisonous. Small boys playing Indian have found this truth, to their wretched unhappiness.

But in May it is full of wild beauty, one of the few purple-striped woods plants; and in Autumn its berries are brilliant. It belongs with the grapeleaf fern and the long-stemmed violets at the foot of the old stone wall. It's as much a part of May as apple blossoms and dogwood bloom against the deep blue sky.

THE fragrance of lilacs is strong on the May morning, and a bouquet of their blooms scents the whole house. They make one glad to be around and have a sense of smell. There's but one thing wrong with lilacs: they are so insistent that they sometimes overshadow May's other fragrances.

Leave the lilacs behind and head for the woods and you will find a whole hillside made sweet by the Canada mayflower, which botanists

R. F. D. BY ADOLF DEHN

identify as *Maianthemum canadense*. It carpets the shadows now, a humble plant with a slender spike of tiny white blossoms more fragrant than the real lily of the valley. Or seek a bank where the wild honeysuckle grows. Some call it the Pinxter flower, and seek it out in early May. At its prime it is magnificently sweet, and some of that sweetness lingers even now, though the crimson-pink petals have withered.

Or merely walk through a meadow, with your nose at attention. There will be the subtle fragrance of the grasses, but there will also be

37

the tang of wild garlic crushed beneath your feet, the pungence of wild mint brushed in passing. Should you come by a farm where somebody has mowed the lawn there will be that pungence of new-cut grass, surpassed only by the fragrance of a hayfield at cutting time, particularly a field of clover or alfalfa.

The country itself, the fresh fields and the damp lowlands, has its fragrance—earthy, leaf-moldy, elemental. It is the smell that brings a gardener to his knees, a farmer to his planting. It is May, lilacs and mayflowers and mint and garlic and honeysuckle, and the good earth itself.

W I L D geranium has been dappling the meadows and the edge of the woodland with bright lavender-pink blossoms that soon will give way to the seed pods from which some call it Cranesbill. And there's a name with poetry in it, the poetry of the woods and fields. You find a lot of that poetry when you call the roll of our wild flowers, for our pioneers, who named them, had a good deal more poetry than organized botany in them.

Jack-in-the-pulpit, for instance. Spotted adder's-tongue. Wake-robin. Trout lily. Blue-eyed grass. Blood root. There's imagination—there's honest poetry—in all of them; and it's good to know them under those old names which, for most of us, were the names by which we first met them.

Who can look at a moccasin flower without seeing the poetic truth of its name? Who can miss the imaginative reality of that little orchid of the lowlands known as snakemouth? And how about Dutchman's-breeches? Yes, and Dutchman's-pipe. Who hasn't gashed a finger on that saw-toothed weed of the buckwheat family that countrymen still call tearthumb?

Monkshood is another of those names packed with poetic truth.

Meadowsweet—who hasn't paused to smell its blooms, which are like miniature apple blossoms and even have some of their sweetness? Goatsbeard, silver everlasting, rabbit-foot clover, milkweed, turtlehead, butterfly weed, calico aster—walk through the countryside and give them their common names and you walk with folk poetry. Poets walked there before you, poets who were farmers and woodsmen and barefoot boys and girls.

IT WAS usually called Decoration Day, out in the Midwest, with the simple directness of country speech. It was hot with the breath of approaching Summer—the first touch of "corn weather"—and it was fragrant with late lilacs and early roses. Small yellow roses, and simple pink ones, bloomed in generous sprays along the picket fences, and huge lilac clusters from the untrimmed bushes in the dooryards. In the fields, as the families drove to the graveyards, there was the drone of bees over the first fat heads of clover. Bees droning and meadowlarks whistling from the fence posts. But otherwise the countryside was strangely hushed.

The Fourth of July would bring celebration, with firecrackers and horse races and baseball and spread-eagle oratory. Old glories would be recounted. Triumphs would be recalled. Families would feast. The bounty and goodness of the land would be praised.

But not on Decoration Day. Defeat would be remembered then, as well as victory; soldiers as well as armies. Life was good, but death was certain; and this was a time to recall that freedom is not cheaply bought, and that peace, which is the end of struggle, lies sweetly on any land. This was a time for long thoughts and humble, thankful thoughts, not for celebration. This was a day for remembering.

OLD MOON BY JOHN S. DE MARTELLY

JUNE.

THERE IS A poignant serenity over the countryside. Sweet clover, tall and heady with fragrance, blooms along the roads, and at dawn and dusk there is the heavy sweetness of honeysuckle. Buttercups twinkle in the sunlight, and in uncut fence corners there is a frosting of first daisies. Corn stands in its pale young green in rows across the hill, and rye lifts its bluish heads to the far bluer sky. The oriole sings in the apple orchard.

I have been out investigating the state of my world, and it measures up extremely well to the expectations one is entitled to in June. Peas are fattening in their pods. Roses cluster around the dooryard trellis, already scattering their first tired petals, and peonies spread their lavish color

An American Year

along the path. Early beans have begun to blossom, and their blooms have the beauty, if not the fragrance, of the sweet peas which I seem so seldom to bring to proper fulfillment. Strawberries are ripening in the June sunlight, and bees buzz through the raspberry patch.

I have even tasted June, in the sun-warm sweetness of strawberries eaten as I plucked them. And I am wondering if that is not half the secret of the flavor in wild strawberries: they ripen at leisure and to their own size, neither hastened nor inflated by man's impatience. Certainly when I choose to eat tame berries fresh plucked I always find the finest flavor in those no larger than my thumb-end, those that have come to ripeness in their own unhurried way.

June, the taste and sight and smell of June, and the calm contentment of having June all around me. And the song of the oriole there in the orchard. That's June, complete.

A PAIR of mourning doves has come to my woods, and their call is like an echo from two thousand miles and more than thirty years away. I know they belong here as much as the tanagers or the towhees, but to me the mourning dove will forever be a bird of the plains. Of a particular valley on the Colorado plains, where John Gault had a big sheep camp and where coyotes lurked in Winter and prairie dogs yelped under the July sun. They belong with devil's-claw and prickly poppy and cactus blooms, not in my birch woods.

John Gault's camp was only a series of broad sheds and low corrals, sprawled on the flat between the buffalo grass hills. In early Spring the ewes dropped their lambs there and the flocks were parceled out to their herders and their respective Summer ranges. At shearing time they came back, flock by flock, to be shorn and branded with black paint and sent to their own ranges again. In Winter it was deserted. It was a place of

ALONG THE HUDSON BY ARNOLD BLANCH

strong sheep smells and, in Spring and Summer, that incessant clamor of blatting ewes, baaing lambs and clanging bells which marks any western sheep ranch. And a place of cottontail rabbits and of doves.

The doves sat on the ridges of the big sheds, lined up like pigeons and a deceptively inviting mark for any marksman. In Spring the herders shot at them with rifles—Gault forbade them to use shotguns on the doves; but relatively few doves went into the herders' pots, for they are not easy targets. In Summer the hawks swooped on them and the air was loud with whistling wings, but doves are not easy prey to hawks,

43

either. For a time I hunted them with a .22 rifle, but the sweet melancholy of their call overcame my hunter's instinct; I turned to the cottontails.

And now that same sweet melancholy echoes through my Hudson Valley woodland, and I can feel once more the July sear of the Colorado sun, see the fried-egg flare of the prickly poppies, smell the rank sheep odor, hear the blatt and baa and the interminable clamor of the bells.

OH, TO be in Bismarck, now that June is here! In Bismarck, says the morning paper's weather report, it was just 43, while New Yorkers were watching the mercury blithely glide up to 89 and cling there. Duluth wouldn't be bad either; Duluth had a high of 47 and a low of 44. Or Denver, which showed a maximum of 65 but retrenched, before the day was over, to 35—only three degrees above the frost line, if you please.

But Bismarck, North Dakota—that's a place to be just now. July will be something else again, on those Dakota highlands, and so will August. The old Missouri River will be fairly steaming and the hilltops will dance like Salome in the sun. But right now the cottonwoods must be in full and twinkling leaf, and the red-shouldered blackbirds must be ka-cheeing in the willow brush. The wheat fields are lying cool and green in the sun, Spring wheat stretching all the way to the horizon. The alfalfa fields must be lovely, too, showing blossom purple and smelling sweet as honey; if not quite yet they soon will be. And in town—yes, even in that capital city of North Dakota—people are sleeping under blankets.

Bismarck happens to be the place where Meriwether Lewis and William Clark camped for the Winter of 1804-5 on their way to the Pacific. They didn't find it exactly a Winter resort. Blizzards came howling down the valley, snow piled deep and the cold nipped the very marrow of their bones. As soon as the thaws came they were on their way again, westward. But if they hadn't been in such a hurry they would have seen what Bismarck could be like in June.

SOME of us used to smile when Grandmother called them "pineys," smile in imagined superior knowledge. They were peonies, of course —huge blossoms that summoned the June bees and colored the whole garden and made sweet the dusk, and finally fell in a profligate showering of petals. Peonies, magnificent flowers that belonged in Grandmother's garden.

What we didn't know was that Grandmother was as right as anybody else; for peony is "piney," and was *paeonia* in the old Latin, and a close approximation of that in solid, back-country English. Grandmother was even more old-fashioned than she knew; but she was right.

And she was right when she dug up her pineys and packed them in a box of New England soil and stowed them in the Conestoga wagon when she went west. Those pineys took root in the rich bottomlands of the Ohio Valley, on the prairies beyond the Mississippi, on the High Plains, in the stony soil of the deserts, on the warm western slope of the Sierra. They meant home to her, in June, wherever she might be.

And still they mean home. Home in June. Sweet peas are lovely, and roses are superb; rhododendron is breath-taking, and columbines are simply beautiful. But peonies are homely, and friendly, and generous beyond belief. Give them half a chance and they are yours for a lifetime; yours in magnificent color and abundance, when June is at its peak.

HOW good it is to step forth into the night after a day of rain and see that the night sky is clear, the stars are gleaming in their accustomed places. A sky that clears by daylight is full of radiance, but when it clears in darkness there is glittering promise in every winking ray of starlight. There is reassurance in such stars, hung in a night sky washed clean and made ready for clear days to come.

Work is done by sunlight; but it is under the stars that great dreams are dreamed. There is warmth and life in the day's sunshine; but it is the stars that lure man's mind to the endless immensity of a universe so broad that tangible reality can never span it.

No night is so dark as a starless night, nor is any life more drab than that of one who has never known the thrill of starlight after storm, the comfort of it and the soothing assurance of stars once more in order. Give a sailor a star to steer by and he will come home to port. Give an airman the company of a star shining clear and you have given him both certainty and direction. Give any man a star on which he can fix his eye and he can reach as far as his imagination points the way.

The rains come, and the dark days of a perverse season; and the sky clears at evening. There is a sweet smell to the darkness, the fresh fragrance of a rain-washed world. And there is the brilliance of a thousand galaxies overhead, starlight in the clear night sky.

IT doesn't require a barefoot boy with investigative talents to find a bumblebee in June. Look in any clover patch or honeysuckle tangle and there he is, neither bashful nor rare. Honeybees may hasten from flower to flower for quick loads of nectar and pollen, but the bumblebee takes his own dignified time, with neither bows nor apologies to mankind and with supreme confidence in his own wings and weapons—particularly his weapons. He can be, but seldom is, a most annoying enemy.

Compared with his honeybee cousins, the bumblebee is a gentleman of leisure. He stores up nothing for the Winter because he dies with the

46

GOLDEN GATE BY ALFRED DEHN

end of the flowery season. He builds only a crude nest and his chief concern is drought. Most of the Summer he merely gorges himself and lives at ease. But his life is far from futile. Pollination of clover flowers is his unsolicited job, but none other does it for him, as Australia and New Zealand learned some years ago. Clover could not be grown successfully there until bumblebees, not native to those lands, were imported and established.

The English call him the "humblebee," which in its literal sense is anything but the truth. His black body with its bright gold band is as

47

much a symbol of arrogant pride as are the plumes of a peacock, and the English know it well. But "humble" in this case is a corruption of "hummer," which explains everything. For the bumblebee is clearly a hummerbee. But a hummer who will not be rushed; he is, and the whole world should know it, a gentleman at leisure for the Summer, the world his home and comfort his lot.

WE knew each other years ago, and now he had returned from almost half a lifetime abroad, including an eternity in an enemy prison camp. He had come up here to relax and to talk, as writing men will, of common friends and uncommon experience. He had seen hell close-up, but this hillside of mine, with its peace and tranquillity, was hard to get used to. Besides, he was city born and raised and full of that restless uneasiness of a stranger in the country.

We sat on the terrace and talked, and the trees made shade patterns around us. Talk lagged, and he asked if this were not an oak above us. He spoke of irises and violets, flowers he knew. Then I took him for a walk up through the birches, and he noted their kinship to the aspens of our western valleys. When we reached the patch where moccasin flowers were opening he was discreetly appreciative. But he could not identify the threefold leaf of poison ivy; he spoke of snakes, and he walked gingerly. I wondered if his stay would not be more of a trial to his taut nerves than a relaxation.

Then a butterfly fluttered past and came to rest on a tuft of panicle dogwood blossom, and he exclaimed, "A swallowtail! A green-clouded swallowtail! Papilio—papilio troilus!" And there was triumph in his voice. My amazement showed in my face, I suppose, for he explained, "I collected butterflies as a boy. Some I caught in a little park just down

48

the street from our house; others I bought from a dealer in specimens. Do you have many around here?" I assured him that we had quite a number, but that I knew them only casually.

And suddenly he was no longer a stranger.

THE countryman is a tolerant fellow, for the most part, taking the wind and the weather as they come and getting along with his neighbors. But this morning he stood in the midst of his strawberry patch and delivered an ultimatum that went something like this:

"You're heading for trouble, Mister Catbird, just as sure as God made little green apples. You're thieving too much. There's a limit to everything, and we can't both have our fill of strawberries out of this garden. . . . You're full of frolic and there isn't another bird in the woods that can hold a candle to you when it comes to putting people in their place. Not even the blue jay. You've got a voice like a wood thrush—when you want to use it; and you've got a voice like a buzz saw. You can make the best of them sound ridiculous, just by singing their own songs in your own way. And jeering, as if to say, 'That pompous old grosbeak makes this sound hard. You see how easy it is! Nyaaaaa!' . . . You're more fun than a paratrooper on twenty-four hour leave, and you've got about as much respect for self-importance as I had twenty-five years ago, when I was loose on the town in a Marine's uniform. I get a kick out of you, and I admit it. . . . But, Mister Catbird, if you don't leave my strawberries alone for a few days, you're going to get a kick out of me. . . . By the way, Tom Davies' berries are ripe too, just in case you haven't heard. And he's got a big patch of them."

A SHOWER came down our valley this afternoon, but it fell on earth so parched by a solid week of heat that the rain rose in a steamy

An American Year

LAZY AFTERNOON BY HANNES BOK

mist as soon as it struck the ground. And this evening it was dry eno
for the boys and me to go out and lie in the tall grass beside the birc
It is the wild grass of the woodlands. Being a plainsman born, I h
such reverence for trees that I cannot cut more than must come do
to make way for my house, my garden and my daily rounds; and I h
neither need nor longing for a lawn, even if one would grow in
deep shade. So the wild grass takes its place, rooting where it will
cept in the flower beds.

We lay and watched the clouds, with their sunset rouge, and at
a breeze came creeping down the hill, a slight breeze that me

ked the leaves on the highest boughs. It was the first real move-
t of air in nearly ten days, and as pleasant a sound as I could recall.
ı it freshened and the birches leaned and all their loose-hung leaves
ın to rustle. I shut my eyes and the sound was like the riffled flow of
Mile Creek in the Sangre de Cristo mountains two thousand miles
y.
The boys have only the faintest memory of Six Mile Creek, but they
recall the swish and whisper of the wind in the pines in the high
ys. And when they mentioned that, I could smell the pitchy fra-
ce of a hundred valleys, see the twinkle of the aspens in the long
t and soft breeze of evening. It is of such little things that big
ories are compounded.
We lay there, each with his thoughts and all with the comfort of
earth at our shoulder blades; and the breeze became a wind, the
s swished and whispered to me, and the heat of many days was
pt down the hillside.

ERE does a wren get all its energy? Not only do the house wrens
build substantial nests and raise two broods a year, but the broods
large, seldom less than four, sometimes twice that number. They
the chicks good care, feed them generously, watch them with
lance until they can fend for themselves. That should be enough
any pair of birds. But all Summer long the cock wren is fussing
ut the bushes building nests, or gathering nest material, that will
er be used.
This energetic pygmy is so intent on clothespin bags—and anything
that hangs on the line—that last year we put out an old pillow

cover and left it there to see what he would do. For two solid months he worked at it, stuffing twigs not only into that bag, but into white pillowcases, work trousers, even bathing trunks. At the end of the season I found that he had stowed half a bushel of twigs in that old pillow cover. Twigs, and nothing else; twigs from the birches, mostly. All through the latter part of June, all of July, and most of August he was busy at it, carrying twigs to the hoard, singing sweetly, amazingly unafraid of me when I went to see how he was coming in this fruitless job.

A pair of them are nesting now in a pin oak outside my study window, an open nest about twenty-five feet from the ground. They nested up there last year, too, and in mid-August one of the youngsters left the nest and couldn't get back. We heard the old birds fussing about and went to see what was wrong; and we found this little fellow there in the bushes, fully feathered but no bigger than my thumb, and yet so active we could not catch it. It spent the night in the bushes and the next day flew away. And within a week all the others in the nest were gone, self-reliant and full of energy and sweet song.

THE earth swings on its trunnions and the Summer solstice nears. Time, like the currents of air and ocean, is forever on the move, and there is no end to the cyclic seasons. The violet bursts its pod and scatters its seed. Maple keys which came spiraling down only a few weeks ago strike root and lift eager leaflets toward the sun. The fledgling robin makes its first flight. The thin horn of a new moon will be hung in the western sky before the week is out.

By such changes do we measure time, and change is endless. A ship stands out to sea in the sluggish flow of the river and its ghost-gray shape is lost in the distance. The moon swings once through its cycle and the ship is there in the harbor again and the river's flow is unchanged. But men have twice crossed an ocean, have traveled with sun and stars and known strange and distant scenes and faces, in that moon cycle.

Tall wheat ripens in the sun on a Texas upland, and men scan the skies for hail clouds and hold their breath at each rising wind. In the Dakotas the chinch bugs cluster like a red stain on the wheat stems, and men pray for a blistering sun to save their fields. The food crop of a nation is in the balance while the length of the day alters by ten minutes.

The earth swings, and the creak of the trunnions can be heard in the drone of a bumblebee, the cry of a gull, the whisper of night wind through the tall green corn in Iowa. And a new moon sits on a ridge where a glacier scarred its way toward the valley only a few aeons ago.

YOU see a whole flock of them lined up on a telephone wire along a country road, notable only for their numbers; and then one takes wing, and another, and suddenly they are all in the air, and you catch your breath at the beauty of their flight. Swallows can do things in the air that ordinarily able feathered fliers would break their necks attempting. These are bank swallows, probably, or cliff swallows, or eave swallows; all are Summer dwellers in this area, and all three varieties are often seen together.

Watch them over a stream or pond in the late afternoon—or the early morning, if you are up to it—and you will see what poetry of motion there is in wings. A swallow can't quite stand still in the air, as a hummingbird does, but it can do everything else; and no hummingbird ever achieved the dives and glides and sideslips and spiral climbs

that a swallow seems to do without effort. Not even a mosquito or w.
gnat can outmaneuver a swallow. And a swallow not only takes its f
on the wing; it gulps it down and takes the next insect without miss
a wingbeat.

A swallow perching is quite undistinguished. On the ground i
definitely ill at ease. The air is the swallow's element, and in so
species the wings are so long that their tips overlap beyond the
That tail, for some reason known only to nature, invariably conta
twelve feathers, never more, never less. Perhaps some apt studen
aircraft design could speculate on that with profit. And some studen
the schedules of nature might do extensive research on the unca.
regularity of the swallow's migration timetables.

But as a layman I will neither speculate nor tabulate my finding
will simply watch, and remember forever the beauty of a fligh
swallows over an evening lake.

I'VE BEEN trying to discourage the wild blackberries at the up
end of the vegetable garden, and they don't discourage easily. Nor d
the viburnum, up there. Or the woodbine or even the fox grape. A
the cinquefoil—the false strawberry—is forever making passes at
bed of tame strawberries, making passes and getting a roothold a
reaching out eagerly for the whole place. The ferns are persisten
that bed, too, though they aren't so eager to get going when I t
them down along the stone wall where I want them to make a feath
mass of green.

There are young oaks in the onion bed, with roots that go dow
foot into the soil, it seems, though they sprouted from acorns onl
couple of months ago. And young birches are darting up among
chives, ash seedlings among the tomatoes. The soil is none too good

fruitful plantings as I make, but for these natives it seems to be
. They would gladly take it over if I gave them one undisturbed
on.

'm a stranger here, a squatter who has carved out a little clearing;
if I go away for a month and leave my clearing untended I shall
n to find how tenuous my foothold really is. Though I use them
, the paths through my woods have to be cleared several times
Summer. I cut a tree and neglect to grub out the roots, and the
time I look at the stump it is hidden in a thicket of second-growth
ts as high as my head.

Nature is neither friendly nor hostile to me; she has no emotions. I
live here, and in comfort, as long as I work at the job. Nature's
tion is growth and change. All I can do is try to guide that growth,
change, to conform to my needs or my desires.

APPROACHING STORM BY RUSSELL LIMBACK

JULY.

JULY IS NOT only a season of the year; it is a season of the mind and memory. Hot days and sultry nights and crashing thunderstorms are a part of July, and to the drone of the bees in the clover fields will soon be added the high-pitched sibilance of the cicada. The tang of ripe cherries and the sweetness of sunning hay belong to July, and so does the cool splash of flowing water where country boys go to swim when corn hoeing or garden weeding has been half finished. Orioles sing in the apple orchard and robins greet the sunrise, and in the evening there is the sweet sadness of the doves, the soft swish of their whistling wings.

But there are Julies other than this. Bees were loud in the clover and the oriole was singing on a July morning when a group of burgesses gathered in the church at Jamestown, there on the river James, to draw up a set of laws for the government of their colony. There was the smell of oozing pitch from the fresh timber, and there was the drone of persistent flies, as those men met; and out of that July meeting, more than three centuries ago, came a simple code of laws by which men might govern themselves. There was a crown governor, to be sure, but there was also the beginning of representative government.

Out of Jamestown, and out of Plymouth, and out of all those other meetings of men who knew in their hearts that man could govern himself, came, in due time, that July in Pennsylvania when farmers from the bee-loud fields came to a city square simmering with city heat and heard the declaration which codified that belief and that philosophy and proclaimed it to the world.

July, sweet and sultry and filled with the sounds and smells of a fruitful season; July, a season of man's remembering, man's rededicating himself to the hopes, the dreams, the aspirations of Julies long gone.

IT WAS the first week in July when he went away, a dark-haired boy who knew and loved this hillside but whose eyes had been looking upward almost half his life. Crows were ugly birds to him, not because of their color or raucous cries but because they were never graceful in flight. Gulls were beautiful, and swallows; they had such easy, natural mastery of the air. Wild geese and ducks were perfect poetry to him, a poetry he knew and understood and worshipped.

His were the winds and the clouds and the stars. He had ax-skill. He could crack a boulder with a maul. Trees grew when he trans-

LOW TIDE BY JULIAN LEVI

planted them, and walls stood when he laid them up. But he could say when we came down through the gray birches and walked among the oaks: "It's good to have a few oaks around. You have to look up to an oak." He knew that when you follow an oak's trunk at night it leads your eyes to the stars; he knew that gray birches lean with the wind and point the way of Winter storms.

His roots were here. The last time he was here we went up to the hilltop where you can see three miles across the valley, and he looked

59

out across the woodland and said, "This is home. I want to come back to land like this." But his heart was there in the sky. He had to fly. He needed wings and power—horsepower. These things he understood almost instinctively. He had to follow the eagles.

It was July when he went away, and I, too, am looking beyond the treetops today, into the depthless blue that so often held his young eyes.

S O M E call it hay, sarcastically; some use the generic term "salad"; some of us speak of it simply as lettuce. But nearly everybody eats it, one way or another. It has been cultivated since ancient times, so long that its origin has been lost; it no longer grows wild even in the East Indies, where it is supposed to have come from in the first place. And today there are more tame varieties than you can shake a stick at, varieties which someone is periodically proclaiming as good for your eyes, your nerves, your digestion or your disposition. But in spite of the faddists, it is still eaten in great quantity.

Some prefer it in the tightly packed head, quartered and doused, sprayed or sprinkled with dressing. And of dressings there is no end, varying from mayonnaise and French dressing through Thousand Island, various cheese concoctions, plain oil and vinegar, to very abstruse combinations of condiments and libations. There are some people who even cook lettuce, thus degrading it abysmally.

The old back-country method, however, still gives honest lettuce a flavor that few professionals seem to achieve. By this method you start with crinkly leaf lettuce, edged with russet and picked in the dew of the early morning. It is kept crisp in the springhouse, in a huge bowl. At a proper time home-cured bacon is fried to its own

THE LAST LOAD BY ALICE STANDISH BUELL

crisp, the lettuce is whisked to the kitchen and bacon and sizzling fat are poured over it. Cider vinegar is then added, and salt and black pepper. And when it gets to the table you may add sugar, if you please, but nothing else.

Each to his taste, of course, but country lettuce wilted with bacon grease and tanged with vinegar is something to remember and come back to when the appetite has a case of the Summer jitters.

JULY is the high noon of the northern year, month of ripened wheat and windrowed hay, of firefly nights and corn growing so fast out in Ioway that you can hear its joints pop in the moonight. July is hot

61

days and sultry nights, rolling thunder and white-fanged lightning. Young eagles take wing in July.

On a July morning men stood in a shore line clearing between the waves and the deep woods of a new land and tended corn planted on new graves to hide their losses from the Indians. Winter was behind them, a Winter of decimation, their first Winter in this new land. But they had drunk this new land's waters, eaten its fruit and flesh; and now their backs were to the ocean and the east, and their long shadows pointed west.

On a July morning men gathered in a city square to hear the words of a declaration, men from the wheat fields and the hay, from the hilltops and the river bottoms. A war was already under way, and now they heard the words, "When in the course of human events. . . ." And some among them heard young eagle wings in the July sky.

On a July morning men marched through the dust of country roads near a town called Gettysburg; and in the sweltering July afternoon men fought and died in the ripening wheat. A battle was won and a war's course decided.

Rain crows clamor of doom in the July heat and cicadas quiver the air with the call of destruction. On the fence rows the honeysuckle gives of its sweetness to the bumblebee and in the dooryard the hollyhock grows high and bright. Wheat ripens in July and corn stands tall, and in the July noon young eagles learn to fly.

THE bean is quite a vegetable. Any kind of bean, yellow wax, green stringless, pole, bush or lima. It's full of vitamins, assorted, and it is packed with nutrients of the protein persuasion. Green, it has a certain succulence. Dried, it can serve as a satisfactory stand-in for absent meat. It even has a beautiful blossom.

A whole garden full of beans would be monotonous, but it would pay its way. Particularly if the gardener had no liking for broccoli or parsnips. What can you do with a parsnip but butter it, or stow it away to be buttered later? Or with broccoli but eat it now or can it, and eat it, substantially the same, later? Even potatoes have their limitations.

But beans! Those who go in for that kind of hay make salad of young bean leaves. When the pods appear, you have green beans by the peck. When the pods toughen and you are full to the brim and quite satisfied with green beans, you can let them run their course and hull them out as dried beans. No canning. No salting down. No pickling. And when the snow flies, you can boil them or bake them or make bean soup of them, soup full of tang and flavor and nourishment that sticks to your ribs.

Yes, the bean is quite a vegetable. And doesn't the bean beetle know it!

BERGAMOT, which some call Oswego tea and others know as bee balm, now lifts its shaggy head of color in the woods and at the roadside, and those who pass by will hear the impatient buzz of a bumblebee and smell the minty tang of the bergamot leaf. Its ragged flower head, almost any shade from scarlet to magenta purple, is the particular delight of bees and butterflies, and its color gleams in the July landscape with a particularly welcome beauty.

An American Year

It comes honestly by its sharp-tanged fragrance, for it is cousin to peppermint and spearmint and catnip and horehound and pennyroyal. It is cousin also to the humble creeper, gill-over-the-ground, which dotted the early Spring with light purple florets so small they were like sparks of color.

Bergamot grows wild, but the borderline between its tame state and its wild is sometimes hard to find. At the edge of an old meadow you may come upon a patch that spilled over, long ago, from the herb garden of a farmhouse now vanished without trace. A mile away it may be marching along a garden fence, thrusting tentative shoots inside toward domesticity. It can make its own way in a forgotten field corner, and it can thrive in luxury in a well-kept dooryard.

But always it is itself, pungently individual, jauntily uncombed and full of color, quite at home in any company. Herbalists once brewed a tea from its leaves, as they did from many mints, and thus came the name Oswego tea. But most of us today are content to smell its pungence, which is as full of the fields as the tang of a sassafras leaf.

WHEAT is ripening in a little field a few miles from here, the only wheat I have seen this year, and I am remembering wheat fields that rippled like a golden sea to the very horizon. I am remembering wheat country, that stretch of the High Plains that reaches from Texas into Manitoba and Saskatchewan; and I am thinking of a wild goose of long ago in New Mexico.

Don Nazario Gonzales lived at La Cienega, near Santa Fe, and, like his neighbors, he grew wheat for his family's needs. One day Don Nazario shot a wild goose, come from somewhere beyond the

OLD MAN TOWNE BOUGHT A NEW SCYTHE BY JOHN S. DE MARTELLY

horizon. Having the curiosity of an unlettered scientist, he opened the goose's crop and there he found seven grains of wheat, a strange, dark, hard wheat with unusually large kernels. He planted those seven grains, and they grew and ripened.

In those distant days the wheat grown in Don Nazario's land was *el trigo Sonoreno*, Sonora wheat from Mexico, a soft grain easily ground into flour by the women using stone metates. But *el trigo Sonoreno* gave only a moderate yield. Don Nazario's goose wheat yielded heavily,

65

and he soon had enough to share with his neighbors. But the hard wheat was difficult to grind in the metates, and soon the women were complaining, not that it was hard but that it made poor bread, its flavor was inferior, it soured easily, the worms got into it. And by thus libeling it they drove it from the fields. Because of their indolence, the hard wheat of heavy yield, so prized today, had to wait another half century.

I am thinking of Don Nazario and wondering how many wild geese are flying over the world today, how many metate users are thinking up false libels for new bounties unrecognized.

THAT crunching sound which is now heard throughout the land is the July lyric of the native epicure, American as Iowa or the Mississippi River. It rises from the measured meeting of tooth and kernel upon the cob. It is tantalizing to hear and a deep delight to indulge. It is the happy munching of the roasting ear.

If the Indian had willed us nothing more, we would be eternally in his debt for that strange, prolific grass we know as corn. It fattens our pork, it primes our beef, it provides the makings for mush and johnnycake and corn bread. It gives us oil and starch and sweetening for our breakfast cakes. But chiefly, in July, it puts roasting ears upon our plates. Roasting ears and fresh, sweet butter, and salt—not even Massasoit could imagine anything more tasty. In July.

There's no need to go into the controversy over varieties; that argument itself pays tribute to the basic virtues of the genus, for it's not a matter of which is good and which is bad, but which is best. The thing to do is make your choice, catch it young, hurry it to the pot and cook it not too long. After that, instinct is the best guide, and etiquette can go hang. For once, buttery fingers are the concomitant of high achievement.

That doesn't cover the ground, by any means. But it does indicate the broad outlines of the subject. . . . Please pass the roasting ears again. And let's all sing a song in praise of that marvelous man, Massasoit!

BOUNCING Bet, the pink that came here from Europe as a garden flower and escaped to the roadsides, has spread itself over the landscape in great banks and patches of pale pink bloom. It lines the road at the foot of my hill, and it has taken over and charitably beautified a onetime dump on the road to town. If it were less profuse it would still be cultivated with care and given a measure of respect, for it has a distinct beauty in a minor way. Its very adaptability and its persistent increase, however, have reduced it to the status of a weed in many places; and when one calls it soapwort, little is added to its doubtful dignity.

It came honestly by the soapwort name, however, and there is no pretense about it. Its root will yield a soapy sap that will produce a lather with notable cleansing qualities. In more remote parts of Europe it was used as a soap substitute for many generations, and probably it is being used as such today.

It was the English who named it soapwort, and it was they who brought its seed to America and gave it its start in the gardens of long

67

ago. Somewhere in the South, however, it picked up another version of that name, My Lady's Washbowl, which indicates that it was used there, too, as a soap substitute in time of need.

But today it is most often known—in these parts at least—as bouncing Bet, and few know that it ever had any particular use. It grows with the horsemint and the poison ivy at the roadside, and even the youngsters usually pass it by. It grows too easily and is too free with its blossoms to make much of a name for itself. All it has is a past and a pale pink flower. And maybe a moral hidden somewhere in its history.

THE first of the season's cicadas have come out to salute the sun—if a cicada's noise can be termed a salute. Anyway, here they are, on telephone poles and in treetops, and they make one realize that Summer is at its peak. Give us enough of them and we shall be hearing about the seventeen-year locusts. If there are only the usual numbers, however, we shall call them harvest flies and let it go at that. The harvest fly, if you are entomologically inclined, is the black-and-green one. The seventeen-year fellows are the longest-lived of insects, and some amateurs say you can tell their age by counting the growth-rings in a cross section. Scientists demur.

Any noisy cicada is sure to be a male of his species. Xenarchus, the Greek poet, once said: "Happy the cicadas' lives, for all have voiceless wives." But he didn't point out that cicadas sometimes burrow as far as twenty feet beneath the surface of the ground to hibernate. Obviously, the seventeen-year variety; it takes all that time to get there and back.

COLORADO SUNFLOWERS BY ADOLF DEHN

Cicadas live on sap. Mostly, however, they just make noise. The only American insect that can compete with the cicada's stridulant song is the katydid, which will be along presently. Cicadas, however, sleep at night; katydids don't. So those who hear the cicadas now had just as well catch up on their own sleep. Maybe that's the cicada's mission in life—to warn of the katydid's coming.

An American Year

WE seldom have brilliant sunsets here, even in the early Autumn when the air should be filled with dust particles which turn the evening light to color. For a long time I kept remembering the western sunsets and scoffing at those who assured me that there was a quiet beauty here at sundown. I was still searching the sky for those Nevada and Arizona evenings when the whole western half of the heavens was aflame, and for those mountain evenings in Colorado when I stood in purple shadow and watched the play of gold and scarlet and cloud-indigo over the peaks.

But now I know what those who talked of quiet beauty were trying to point out. My hillside slopes east and my house is well banked with tall trees, but if I go down the road to the turn where I can look across the valley just as the sun is touching the treetops behind me I can see evening spread across a four-mile expanse. The far ridge is well wooded, and the valley is filled with swamp maples; and at that hour of day when the light is long and golden the shadows are deep and the highlights strong. It is a tranquil scene with a rich patina of dying sunlight, and often there is just enough mist in the air to give it that faint touch of mystery and uncertainty of line which so enhance these eastern hills.

The hilltop in the old pasture also offers particular sunset beauty. At its western rim is an old hedgerow, maples and tulip poplars and an ambitious fringe of gray birches. At a certain time of evening the sun comes streaming through those trees in long lines of glowing silver that light the tall grass with the cool flame of sunset. It, too, is a quiet beauty. But to see it I must lower my eyes from the heavens to which I was long accustomed to look for the sunset.

NOW come the dog days, and I still hear it said that this is the time of year when ponds grow poisonous, dogs go mad and snakes are blind

VALLEY OF THE WISCONSIN BY JOHN STEUART CURRY

and doubly vicious. The persistence of such superstitions explains Merlin and his glib disciples. Incidentally, it also shows, in this instance, how directly our culture—if that is what it is—stems from ancient Rome.

With the old Romans, most of July and the fore part of August were full of heat. Lacking adequate sanitation, many Romans fell ill and died. And, as in all countries, those hot days brought great discomfort to dogs, which ran rabid through the streets. Rome's official stargazers were ordered to seek the reason for such seasonal phenomena, and

71

they found—as the Greeks and Babylonians had found before them—that the star they called Canicula, the Little Dog, at that time of year rose in conjunction with the sun. With their peculiar logic, they reasoned that Canicula was to blame, and thus came the *dies caniculares*. The dates were July 3 to August 11.

Had our habits and superstitions come from Egypt instead of Rome, however, the dog days would probably be a time of beneficence, for the Egyptians knew that Canicula—they called it Sirius—came into conjunction with the sun at the time when the Nile rose in flood. The Nile's flood was the source of Egypt's agricultural plenty, so Egypt's dog days were hailed with thanks and, indeed, marked the beginning of a new year.

Of such flimsy thread are many of our folkways woven. The wonder to me is not that so many absurdities persist, but that we have rid ourselves of so many that dogged our daily lives through the murky past.

T H E ant is an insect. It has a thick-shelled head, a thorax to which six tireless legs are attached, an abdomen of limitless capacity. Its mandibles can and do chew and bite at will. It lives in colonies, in the earth, in old stumps, in house beams or in bags of sugar in my pantry. Some entomologists insist that the ant is very smart; many amateurs are equally insistent that the ant merely persists in its venerable, stubborn way.

Some who have spent a good deal of time studying ants say that they have a socialistic economy. The observant amateur may wonder—I do—why no Socialist has ever sued for libel. The ant's social organization seems to consist of a large group of female workers, almost as many drones, a standing army which is forever looking for trouble, crowds of slaves, and a queen who does nothing but perpetuate the ant race. That part of an ant's time not spent in eating or looking for food seems to be spent in annoying the neighbors, insect or human.

The ant is supposed to hear sounds beyond the range of the human ear. That is why the ant knows you are preparing to war on the ants in the pantry before you even make a move in that direction; it hears the thought clicking through your brain. The ant is also believed to have a remarkable sense of smell. That is why the ants gather in the pantry and dance in glee while you are buying sugar at the store two miles away; they smell it coming.

Ants fertilize flowers, quite unintentionally, while they are looking over the pollen situation. They pasture their herds of aphids on the best of the cabbage plants. They sharpen their mandibles on the under side of the front steps. Thank goodness, they also eat sodium fluoride.

THE SWIMMING HOLE BY CHARLES WILSON

AUGUST.

AUGUST IS one of the hottest months of the northern year, so hold your breath and see that the fan is in order. It is also one of the longest months, and sometimes it seems even longer. But it brings roasting ears and ripe tomatoes in such abundance that nobody can eat them all. That's why we have tomato juice and ketchup—thank August for that.

Sometimes it rains in August; August thunderstorms are masterpieces of bluster and bombardment. And sometimes August is bone-dry and full of dust, and we would gladly swap the whole of it for one rainy March week end.

There isn't a holiday worth mentioning in August, but along toward the middle of the month there is a sizable shower of shooting stars. Of somewhat lesser importance is the anniversary of the first talking motion picture and of Blondine's hike across Niagara on a tightrope.

August also brings katydids, elderberries, blackberry pie, and golden-rod. It brings dog days and a bilious tinge to back-country swimming holes. Watermelons ripen in August, sometimes and in some places, and watermelon pickles simmer on the stove in an unbearably hot farm kitchen; the fragrance is something no farm boy ever forgets. Before there were combine-harvesters, August was threshing time in the small-grain country, a season the farm wife who cooked the meals for the threshers also never forgets.

August is just another thirty-one days of concentrated Summer, but it certainly gets one in condition to appreciate Fall when it comes. Good old August—we'll take it, and some of us will like it.

THOSE dark, swift wings hovering over the garden these August evenings are moths, not hummingbirds as they appear at first glance in the dusk. Hawk moths, some call them, or sphinx or hummingbird moths. They are easily mistaken for hummingbirds, for they are about the same size both in body and wing span and they, too, haunt the deep-throated flowers and hover over a blossom on wings that beat so swiftly that no eye can follow them. But they are true moths, and at one stage of their development they have been voracious hornworms feeding on tobacco or eating the heart out of ripening tomatoes.

As moths, however, they are full of quiet beauty, olive green or gray or wood brown with patterned wings whose detail is quite invisible until you have captured one and stilled those wings. And then, too, you can see why the sphinx chooses the petunias, moon flowers and the Nicotiana at which to feed. It has a snout or sucking tube as long as your finger which is coiled like a nautilus shell there beneath its eyes when not in use. When it is feeding, that snout can be thrust into the depths of any floral trumpet to reach the nectar.

The sphinx seldom comes to batter its life away against a pane or screen when the lights have been turned on inside the house. Usually it is the Luna moth which comes, with its light green wings, or the Cecropia or Polyphemus, yellow or brown or delicate shades of red. In terms of beauty, all three surpass the sphinx. But the sphinx probably outlives them because it has a lesser degree of light-madness, a greater concentration on the necessities of life. And if there's a moral here, it started with a green hornworm gnawing at a ripening tomato; nature's morals, if any are to be found, have some very strange obliquities.

A FEW days ago I was annoyed by the ants raiding our sugar supply. Yesterday I found that carpenter ants in the root cellar had raided two jars of blueberry preserves, carving their way through the protecting paraffin. This morning red ants are on the march past the front door, an endless column of them hurrying south along the flagged terrace.

We watched the column, first in wonder, then in awe, and we followed it back, seeking its source; but we lost it in a tangle of undergrowth fifty yards from the house. Then we followed it forward and found a war in progress. At the far end of the terrace the red invaders converged upon an underground colony of black ants. Even as we watched, some of the reds plunged into the entrances and some of the blacks came scurrying out to face the onslaught aboveground. But the struggle seemed hopeless, for the blacks were outnumbered a hundred to one. They fought, but even while the battle was on one contingent of the reds was making off with pillaged eggs, and now a double column hurried along the terrace—one column racing to the attack, the other hurrying away with plunder.

There was such a mass of ants that one had to concentrate on a small area to see the action in any detail. I chose a six-inch square and there I saw ten ant-to-ant combats in progress at once. I am no entomologist, but it seemed to me that each embattled ant's purpose was to maim its opponent by cutting off its legs or its antenna. Mandibles were the weapons, and maimed combatants littered the ground or ran in frantic circles as I watched. But the outnumbered blacks seemed to leave as many red victims as they received casualties, and it became clear to my superior judgment that the whole war was being waged on something like the totalitarian theory—engage the enemy with overwhelming numbers, hold his army in combat, and send in your looters to strip his land, enslave his youth and decimate his future armies.

THE ant war reached a pause just before dusk last evening, but before midmorning it was under way again. When I went to look at the battleground I had watched yesterday, however, I found more red victims than black. But I do not trust that observation, for when I watched closely I saw a horde of tiny black ants, no more than a thirty-second of an inch long, scavenging the battleground. I should have liked to watch these scavengers, but the red invaders came on in even greater numbers than yesterday, and I had the uneasy feeling that I was watching a microcosm of human history in the fifth century. Or in this century, for that matter.

Today we found the column's source, finally following it back through the woods, over the stone wall, into the old pasture and to a

THRESHING BY ADOLF DEHN

slightly mounded grass patch that looked as though a mole had heaved it. It is just over a hundred yards from the house, and gauging an ant's size against that of a man I judge that distance as the equivalent of nearly twenty miles. Fill a twenty-mile road with troops fifteen abreast, move those troops at motorcar speed, keep that road filled for sixteen hours—and you have some conception of this invasion.

I have seen fossils of ants in the Oligocene deposits at Florissant, Colorado, and there seems to be agreement that they have been on this earth uninterruptedly for at least fifty million years. I can believe that, and I can believe that only a slight shift in nature's balance would deliver this whole world to the mercy of the ants, though I doubt that there is any quality even remotely resembling mercy in those armored heads and implacable mandibles.

It takes little imagination to bring a tightening of my belly muscles in horror when I watch such an ant column as this one which moves endlessly across my terrace. That is why I get out the spray gun, the hose and the ant poison, not frantically but with grim determination.

BONESET is almost ready to open its white flower-heads and stand in competition with the more colorful Joe-pye weed, its pink-topped cousin. The two of them grow together in the margin of my moist woodland, along with New Jersey tea and cattail in sparse clumps and jewelweed in great profusion. This season the Joe-pye weed, for some reason, has gone completely rank; one clump stands so tall that when we took a carpenter's rule and measured it, we found that, in the boy's words, it was "six feet and fifty-eight inches high."

The boneset, at its present best, stands only about five feet, but its bud heads are lavish enough to delight any of the old herbalists. The flowering tops and the upper leaves were gathered and dried in the days when herbs were a stand-by in the country home, and a bitter tea was brewed from them. This tea, taken cold and in small doses, was regarded as a stimulating tonic; in large doses it was a purgative. If the family was stricken with colds, sore throat or malarial fever, the brew was administered hot and was believed to give prompt relief.

Perhaps it also had some relation to the treatment of broken bones,

but I have yet to confirm such use or to find any other obvious reason
for the name boneset. Some call it thoroughwort, and the supposition
is that this name comes from the leaf shape, each pair being joined at
the base and the stem appearing to skewer them; that, of course, leads
one back to obsolete English on an interesting path but one full of traps
and confusions. Follow the botanists and you get there more directly,
for they call it *Eupatorium perfoliatum.*

LIFT your eyes to the nighttime heavens now if you would see the
lights of infinity. The Perseids are darting through the skies, leaving
fiery trails of stardust. Somewhere out there in the tremendous depths
of space the twin fires of creation and dissolution are crackling with
cosmic showers of sparks.

As far back as the legends of man can reach, the Perseids have been
flaming through the skies at this time of year. Those who know most
about the stars and their courses tell us that they probably are the debris
of some comet which once fell into the orbits of the solar system. They
are a comet's tail, left wandering through the heavens until its fires shall
have burned down to their last cinder glow. We who watched them as
children will watch them as grandfathers, and so too shall our own
grandchildren watch; and but a moment of infinity shall have passed.

Out there, they are the dust of creation, aflame with the fires of the
universe. But bring such a meteor down to earth in the form of a
meteorite and it reveals itself as kin of the rocks and hills we know, kin
even of the soil in our own garden. For there is a community of the stars
and planets which is as yet an unsolved mystery.

Watch the Perseids, and wonder; but before wonder has thinned
away to doubt, turn to the north. Turn from the meteoric death-trail

there in infinity and see the Pole Star, the undying light of the northern sky. And know that while meteors crackle across the heavens and die in outer darkness, the universe continues in its eternal rounds.

THE evening primroses are opening now on their tall stalks, beautiful golden yellow and scented strongly, a lemon scent with a special sweetness. I like to watch them at dusk, when the sphinx moths come to share this sweetness, or just before sundown when the blossoms open, sometimes so swiftly that I can see the petals unfolding, one by one. Each bloom is open one night and fades under the next day's full sun. But others follow in succession, so the night is sweet with primrose fragrance for several weeks on end. They grow wild, and we encourage them to grow plentifully.

We encourage them for their own beauty and sweetness, but I have another reason. They take me back to a certain valley on the Colorado plains of my boyhood. There, at this time of year, the giant evening primroses, which the botanists call grandiflora, opened in the dusk and made the evenings a time of wonder and delight. I found them first by accident, for we were all strangers there, discovering flowers we had never known. The moths led me to them, and I mistook the moths for hummingbirds.

They grew on stems that lifted their flowers less than a foot from the ground, and their foliage was nothing to catch one's eye. But when dusk came, when the bullbats were crying through the upper air and the coolness began to move down the valley, one could stand and watch the primroses open their giant petals, as I watch these lesser primroses open theirs. My prairie primroses were four inches across, and their fragrance could be sensed fifty yards downwind.

82

I found them first the Summer I was ten years old. I can still smell their sweetness in the dusk, as I watch the moths hover at these primroses here in my eastern woodland.

CONSIDER the wheelbarrow. It may lack the grace of an airplane, the speed of an automobile, the initial capacity of a freight car; but its humble wheel marked out the path of whatever civilization we still have. Particularly that phase of it which leads down Main Street, through the front gate, around the house and into the back garden. Or simply from the barnyard to the garden and the root cellar. It also led the way up Fifth Avenue, across State Street and even through Piccadilly Circus; but that's another story.

The story I prefer is a simpler one. It deals with rocks and roots and hunks of sod and bags of lime. It includes dead leaves and lively onions, old compost and new potatoes, seedling flats and spades and rakes, squash and pumpkins and outsize heads of cabbage. And two wooden handles, two calloused hands. It makes the rounds of March mud and May rains, July sun and August thunderstorms, October harvest and November frost. It goes places without ever getting far from home.

Like faith, the wheelbarrow can move mountains. A few drops of oil can silence its loudest complaint. In Spring it is a thing of beauty, particularly if it is both new and red. In Summer it is a challenge to human endurance. In Fall it is—sometimes—a cornucopia. Always it is there, needing only human companionship and cooperation to get things done.

Best of all, it is shaped to its purpose. When the sun is at its height, the garden bench is far away and human energy has receded to the very

AUGUST SHOWERS BY DOUGLAS GORSLINE

neap, the wheelbarrow waits with welcoming arms and recumbent seat. No rock, no bag of lime, no harvest from the fertile earth ever fitted the contours of the wheelbarrow as well as the weary frame of its owner.

T H E sumac catches my eye each time I go up the road, for there is a bank of it at the upper end of my place, the humble smooth sumac inter-mingled with the tall, airy staghorn. Just now their leaves form sworls and star patterns that delight the eye, and I wonder why no photographer has caught the beauty of their soft lines and their elusive play of light on leaf and stem, light that is never twice the same.

When first I saw this bank of sumac by moonlight I thought I had unwittingly passed by, in daylight, some bright gleaming row of white-

84

blossomed shrubs. Then I knew it was moonlight reflected from the underside of the pendant leaves; but the effect was pure magic. It is even more pronounced when I drive down the road at night, for those leaves pick up the gleam of my car's headlights and give it back to me in a dazzling burst of silver blossom.

When Fall begins to creep across the land, of course the sumac is the first to know it. Some impatient sumac stems even take on a touch of scarlet the last week in August. But the full beauty comes when the birches turn to tarnished gold. Then this bank is magnificent, and I wish it faced my house instead of the road, that I might watch its subtle change from faint scarlet through all the tones of red to deepest crimson.

True, there are disreputable members of the sumac family—poison ivy and poison sumac and poison oak; but what family does not have its renegades? Indeed, I seem to be a renegade myself when I call it "shoomack," unless I am among countrymen of my own tongue. But shoomack it is to me, and beautiful any day in the year, even in the nakedness of its Winter groping toward the sky.

JOE-PYE weed now makes the moist lowlands and damp waste places glow with lavender-crimson beauty. Weed it is called and weed it may be, but it has a history that goes back more than two thousand years.

Eupatorium is the generic name, which takes it back to the days when Eupator Mithradates was King of Pontus. This particular Mithradates was full of knowledge of the woods and fields, and he knew the simple remedies that grew there to ease human ills. For fevers, he took a magenta-flowered plant from which he brewed an infusion that brought relief.

Long later an Indian "yarbman" in New England came out of the woods with simple remedies from nature. Backwater settlers, ridden by the ills of that time and place, found good in his potions and superstitions. They found particular relief from typhus fever in the remedy he contrived from this lusty, magenta-headed plant of the lowlands. Joe Pye was the Indian's name. Inevitably, the plant became known as Joe-pye weed.

So King and "yarbman" are both remembered, brothers in lore and discovery in the open fields. The plant, weed of the waste places and wildling still, is their obscure memorial. Its flower is magenta, a compromise between crimson and lavender, but it has strange overtones of purple at times. But not royal purple, even in overtone. For this plant is American to the very root; it belongs to Joe Pye, the "yarbman," not to Eupator.

THOSE who fish for bass and trout loftily ignore the very existence of the catfish, and perhaps properly so; he is not for them. But the countryman, the man who can tell a channel cat from a bullhead or a mud cat, knows there's fun as well as food in catfish water.

You can fish for cats either day or night, but country boys—and men too—like to go in the evening. There's something about a deepening night on a pond or stream bank that gets into a country fisherman's emotions and settles there most pleasantly. For such an evening you take a lantern, a can of worms, a light pole and, if you are fishing from a boat, a hand line. And take a congenial companion, a quiet conversationalist, not a chatterer.

Once on the water or beside it, you bait your hook generously with worms; night crawlers are best—those big fellows that abound at the edge of a barnyard. You let the bait sink in promising water and keep

SUMMERTIME BY AARON BOHROD

an attentive finger on the line or pole. If the catfish are there, one will find your worms; and if he is of a respectable size you will know it. But you'll soon bring him in. Experienced hands will know how to handle him, how to avoid the sharp horns with which he is armed, how to disengage the hook; inexperienced hands will soon learn—or decide that catfishing is not for them.

Dusk deepens and soon the night is there to enjoy. This is what you came for, as much as the fish themselves—the starlight, the wind in the willows, the night call of the heron, the gleaming wake of a muskrat in

87

the water. But you don't talk much about these things, not to outsiders. You tell them—if they ask—that you had a mess of cats by midnight, that you skinned them, soaked them in salt water and had them fried for breakfast. Good? Well, a catfish fisherman enjoys them. That's about all you can say—to an outsider.

MAYBE it's imagination, but the trees seem to be looking tired. The pristine green of May and June is a bit faded and dusty, and a good many leaves are tattered and brown at the edges. Autumn is just around the bend.

You see Summer somewhat frayed along the roadsides, too, where ragweed stands rank and full of pollen. Most of the grass has gone to seed. Joe-pye weed with its pink plumes, and ironweed with its purple heads, lord it over everything else, with goldenrod for a background. Look beyond the fences and you see ragged corn tassels and hay browning in the stack.

The wild berries are mostly gone, and the wild grapes are coloring. Apples blush, the early ones, and the late ones are fat and green on the bough. Even the dust seems to hang longer in the air, and sunsets take on more color. If you get up early enough, you will see the same haze at sunrise—which now comes at an almost civilized hour of the morning. It's the haze of the whole Summer's dust.

But mostly it's the trees that seem tired—the trees and such bushes as the sumac, where an occasional leaf has already turned. They have done the bulk of their Summer's business and it won't be long before they are putting on their war paint and full regalia for the Indian Summer ceremonials. There will be a few more weeks to wait, but the peak of Summer is past. The trees are beginning to show the signs of a hard season's work.

88

O N E thing about the zinnia: you needn't pamper it. Give it a root bed, sunlight and a fair start, and it will make its own way. It responds to care and cultivation, but it makes few demands. And with half a chance a bed of zinnias will brighten the end of August as few other flowers. It will brighten the fore part of August, too, but there is more competition then.

Its colors are strong, old-fashioned colors with little subtlety. Botanists and breeders have done things to its shape—twisting its petals and quilling them and even fringing them—but it remains a zinnia for all that. Not even the specialist can alter the zinnia scent, which any old-fashioned gardener can recognize in the dark of the moon. And its generosity is magnificent; cut one bloom and two will replace it.

Some call it a rank and weedy plant and liken it to the sunflower. But no matter. There's a relationship all right; there's kinship, too, with the big daisies and, in lesser degree, with the asters. They're all composites with disc centers fringed by ray petals. But the zinnia needs no apologies. It holds its bright head high, in the garden or the decorator's bowl, and speaks for itself.

My reference books say its name honors "the German botanist Zinn." But I have been told by one who bears the name Zinn today that the plant really was named for Johann Gottfried Zinn, personal physician to Catherine, wife of England's King George III. Dr. Zinn, who seems to have been an early brain and eye specialist, also gave his name to that part of the brain known as the Zone of Zinn.

The plant, whatever the source of its name, is as native to this continent as the pumpkin. Mexico and our own Southwest cradled it and the early Aztecs knew and honored its beauty. Stout Cortez found it flourishing in the legendary gardens of Montezuma when he captured the City of Mexico. It still has the glow of the southern sun in its petals.

BELMONT FARM BY SAM THAL

SEPTEMBER. DOG

days are over, and here comes September. Not Autumn, yet; simply September, which can be as sweltering as mid-July and as chill as late October, and usually manages to be both. Flowers still bloom in September, but sumac and swampland maples give them the lie by turning a gorgeous Autumn scarlet. Birds that I haven't seen or heard since June come trooping back with their songs; and birds that have made themselves at home here all Summer go gallivanting off to Florida on the first inviting breeze.

September is as perverse and indecisive as March; but it is much easier to live with. Unless it goes completely berserk, even its chilliest evenings demand no more than a hearth fire. And when it reverts to

An American Year

Summer type we can shift back to lightweight clothes without ransacking every closet in the house. Its moonlit nights are lovely, and some of its days are among the year's best.

Youngsters have their grudge against it; but so do the teachers, so that score is evened off. Farmers think well of it, for it marks a season's end, with a harvest and another cycle completed: shocks of corn and heaps of pumpkins will dot the fields before September's gone. And the woodlands will be a blaze of Autumn beauty.

Meteorologists can explain September in terms of the shifting sun and the equinox. That's all very well; but September is more than thirty days of weather. It's a break in the seasons, a turning point in the year. And no one can explain September to me in terms of temperature and prevailing wind; there's no savor to that, and September is savory to every sense I possess.

CLUSTERS of gray berries are ripening on the ruddy stems of the red osier dogwood, and the light blue of silky cornel berries can be seen nearby. And if I were a contemporary of Dan Boone I should be gathering my materials for kinnikinnik. I should be snipping twigs from the red osier and the silky cornel, and I should be choosing small, smooth leaves from the sumac and looking for bearberry vines from which to pluck a few handfuls of thick green leaves. I might also be gathering the leaves of the arrowwood viburnum, here in the East, or of the manzanita if I were in the Southwest. All these things would go into my kinnikinnik.

Kinnikinnik is an Algonkian word meaning mixture, and it perfectly describes what went into the ceremonial pipe. The recipe varied from area to area and even from season to season. One more or less standard kinnikinnik contained the scraped inner bark of the silky cornel and of the red osier dogwood, dried and sorted, and the dried leaves of bearberry and sumac. To this might be added arrowwood leaves, manzanita leaves, in some instances willow leaves.

The ingredients were thoroughly dried and mixed. Then they were rubbed and crumbled between the hands to reduce them to a proper fineness for the pipe bowl. This rubbing between the palms inspired the name given to the mixture by the French *voyageurs,* who called it *bois roulé,* rolled wood; it would seem that the kinnikinnik the *voyageurs* knew had a high percentage of bark.

Sometimes the mixture also contained the tobacco we know, but not always and not much. When it did, it usually was the white man who added it. The Indian preferred pure kinnikinnik.

T H E first week in September is no time to begin an inventory of Autumn; but any one with half an eye has surely seen the signs that Summer has lost its grip. It will be another two weeks and more before the calendar acknowledges the turn, and the frost that makes the change official should be even farther in the offing. But the eye and the ear can't be deceived for long.

Flashes of scarlet gleam from the green depths of the sumac clumps. On old stone walls there is the deep red of impatient woodbine already turning. Autumn asters have begun to frost the meadow. The birches on the uplands are dusting the earth with tarnished golden leaves and one can begin to see the blue sky through their feathery tops. Bunch-grass plumes show bronze and copper, and fern clumps, so jaunty a month ago, begin to droop. Berries ripen on scarlet stems of the pokeweed and the flattened fruits of the grapeleaf viburnum turn purplish-black.

An American Year

The birds haven't resumed their song yet, as they will when they are rallying for the trip south in a few more weeks, but in the cicada sunlight the jays and the crows make the days seem as Autumnlike as October. And the crickets are chirping.

So much has to happen in the woods and fields between blistering August and frosty November that Autumn hasn't much time to waste. It will still play at being Summer on a good many days, but it will only be playing at it, really.

A COOL rain falls this evening, a rain that came up in midafternoon with a great thundercloud and a long bombardment and finally settled down for the night. And I am thinking of September rain in Kansas and the greatest congregation of kangaroo rats I ever saw.

We were driving south across western Kansas, down to Cimarron and Dodge City. Jack rabbits and mirages had led the way for hour after hour along the dirt roads of the hot plains; and then a great bank of gray cloud heaved itself out of the south and the rain swept over us on the wings of a high wind. It was a wind that literally blew us into the ditch three times. But at sunset the wind died away and the rain became a gleaming silver portiere in the car's lights. And the road became sand instead of clay.

One of the boys saw them first at the roadside. He had no more than spoken when we all saw the host of little silvery ghosts leaping and frolicking ahead of us. We drew up and watched, and there were dozens of kangaroo rats in a kind of ecstatic rain-dance there in our headlamps' beams. They were round-eared, round-faced little fellows with glinting eyes and gleaming, silvery bellies, long, tufted tails and legs like true

94

GRAIN ELEVATORS BY DALE NICHOLS

kangaroos. But they were no more than twice the size of a field mouse.

We sat there in the rain and watched for perhaps five minutes, then drove on thinking we had been especially privileged. But those dozens we had seen were only the outriders of that road's fantastic population. For the next ten miles they were forever in the beams of our lights, dancing in a light-mad frenzy. There were thousands of them, perhaps hundreds of thousands.

They must be dancing along that road tonight.

An American Year

BURRS, big and little, are ripening. If I walk along the roadside or across the fields, I have to spend half an hour afterward getting them off my clothes, even longer if I wear tweeds instead of denim. But before I consign the pests to the fire, to make sure they will not be dooryard neighbors next year, I like to line them up, kind by kind, and study their hooks and spurs and barbs and spines.

Tick trefoils are a particularly disappointing nuisance. A month ago the trefoils, which are a lesser member of the legume family, had sprays of miniature lilac sweet pea flowers. Now those flowers have matured into a compound seed pod like a miniature of the sickle bar on a farmer's mower. Brush against that pod and it breaks into little flat three-cornered green pods, each covered with barbed bristles. I hear some people call these beggar-ticks, but the true beggar-tick is like a small brown sunflower seed with twin horns at the top, each horn barbed. And it comes from a relative of the marigold, one of the composites with a sunflower-like head full of the prickly little nuisances. We used to call them beggar's-lice.

Another pesky little burr—one which fairly burrows into tweed—is the tiny brown seed of the enchanter's nightshade, which comes from an unworthy member of the evening primrose family. It is completely covered with hooked bristles and is a first-class nuisance.

I've found little burdock and no cockleburs. How well I remember the cockleburs of the Midwest, fat as a thumb and barbarously armed. There are a few sandburs, but their prickles seem not half so sharp as they did in barefoot days.

None of them, excepting the tick trefoil, is worth a second look when in flower. But they are marvelous examples of nature's ingenuity. Some seeds she gives to the wind, some she gives to the birds, but the burrs she simply endows with stick-to-itiveness.

September

T H E frost is not yet on the pumpkin—not by quite a spell, we hope; but the fox grape is on the vine and the Autumn berry is on the bush. Most of the berries are still green, for, unlike the breakfast-table berry, their season comes late. They reach their prime just in time to fatten the birds for their southward journey or for the Winter here at home. But they make the late Summer woods a place of discovery.

The fat berry cluster of the Jack-in-the-pulpit is already showing signs of its ultimate lacquer red. The dogwood of the showy blossom lifts its fruit to the sun for rouging; the panicle dogwood and the red osier, of humbler bloom, are already flaunting wax-white berries on blushing stems. Solomon's seal dangles tiny eardrops in the wind. Dark, heavy umbels of the elderberry are already past their prime, but the inkberries and the purple bounty of the pokeweed hang deceptively enticing.

Bittersweet has fat pink fruit awaiting only the frost to split its outer hull and delight the eye. Benzoin, which cast a yellow haze over the lowlands with its tiny April blossoms, is ripening the fat berries that gave it the name of spice bush; Great-grandmother used those berries in place of allspice. Almost unnoticed, the lowly partridgeberry creeps among the shadows with its green dewdrops that will gleam so valiantly red against the Winter snow.

They are all in fruit—the numberless viburnums, the snowberries, the winterberries, the bayberries which yielded fragrant wax for backwoods candles. They won't reach their height of beauty for another month or more, but many of them will be gleaming in the woodlands long after the leaves around them have blazed with color and gone their Falltime way.

T H E asters were named for the stars, and in September one might believe the reason was their number rather than their shape. For they come now along every roadside, in every meadow, on rubbish heaps and in the edges of the woodland. They come like a cloud, a foam of bloom that covers the whole landscape. For a time they take the eye off the leaves that have already begun to drift down from the trees; this is their day, their season in the sun.

Try to count them and you run out of numbers. Try to classify them and you run out of names. They range from miniatures that demand a glass for study to gaudy fellows a couple of inches across. Their petals vary from deep lavender to pure white, and some of them even have a touch of purple. Count the petals and you may come out anywhere between six and twenty. And their leaves vary from the most parsimonious little slivers of green to heart-shaped spans as big as your hand.

They are as varied as Americans—and most of the asters of the world are natives of America. The big, showy garden varieties, to be sure, are chiefly of Chinese origin. But do they grow wild? Do they swarm over the meadows and along the roadsides? They do not. They cling to the luxury of man-made gardens, and they all too often have a hothouse temperament.

But the natives—there's your September glory! Frost on the meadows when there's not yet a trace of frost in the air. Blossom at its height when the leaves are already falling. A veritable Milky Way strewn across the American landscape.

THE FIRST of the sour gum leaves are turning color, and I thank fortune that I did not mark all the sour gums when the builders moved in here to put up our house some years ago. I marked one, between the house site and the road, carefully explaining that it was not to be cut; and a week later I found a pile of lumber where it had been. Thereafter I painstakingly marked gray birches, and the sour gums escaped.

September

As trees, they are full of twisted branches that seem uncertain where they are going—sometimes starting on one side of the trunk and ending on the other, sometimes heading for the sky and then turning abruptly earthward. The whole effect is full of surprises and unexpected lines, particularly when the leaves have fallen and the gray branches stand clean against the Winter sky.

But the sour gums are beautiful, in leaf or out. In Spring each leafbud opens into a tuft of green until the whole tree is fairly tasseled. Another week and the almost waxen leaves are widespread. Then come the tiny flowers, resembling the blooms of the panicle dogwood of which it is cousin; you scarcely see the blossoms—so small they are and so green— but you smell their sweetness and you hear the bees which come in veritable swarms. A sour gum in blossom time is, one can truthfully say, a mass of sweetness and sound.

And in Autumn it is a mass of color—rich, deep orange-red that stands out vividly against the yellow of the birch and the ash. A sprig of sour gum in full color lights a whole room; best of all, it holds its color for weeks. New Englanders call it the pepperidge tree, and Southerners use the Indian name tupelo. But to me it is the tree of that lilting old fiddle tune, "Possum on a Gum Stump."

T H E notes of a flute came from somewhere down the valley this evening. I have no idea who was playing it, or where, but those few notes took me back more than twenty years and set me down in a live oak grove in southern Mississippi.

We had crossed the Big River that morning and struggled over red

99

NO FENCE LAW BY W. R. LOCKE

clay roads deep with mud, and toward evening we came out onto this flatland covered with live oaks hung with Spanish moss. There was not a house in sight nor could we hear any sounds of habitation, so we drew up in a little opening in the woods and made camp. Dusk filtered through the bearded trees and an orange moon came out and frogs thumped the night. Then we heard the flute.

First came a few trial notes like a hesitant bird song. Then came a

100

trill and a run which caught a melody, held it, embroidered it. The notes danced and bubbled. They were a boy whistling homeward from work, a girl laughing in the moonlight, an old man remembering his youth. Then they were a sobbing cry of melancholy, all minors; and at last the original melody reappeared—clear, simple, haunting, like nothing I had ever heard. And it did not end; it simply died away into the soft sigh of the night wind.

The next morning, when we had stowed our gear and were about to leave, a little dark man came walking down the road, paused and smiled a greeting. I asked about the road ahead, but he had never been five miles from there and a map was a complete mystery to him. So he bade us well and went on down the road, whistling as he went. The melody he whistled was the one we had heard in the moonlight—the flute melody— simple, haunting. It haunts me still.

N O W that the leaves have thinned out a bit, I can see from my study window how another season's growth has changed this landscape. Up there where I cut a clump of gray birches last Spring to let a little more light and sunshine through the woods I see six sturdy shoots grown up from the root. I cut three trees and six new ones have come to take their place. The wind has blown the top out of a tall birch nearby, and I must take down the stub; but it, too, will be replaced in triplicate unless I take out the root.

Just above the wall here I see a dozen ash seedlings, grown high as my waist over the Summer. Two or three more undisturbed years and they would be a young thicket. There are young tulip trees two feet high at the foot of the wall, not ten feet from the house. I didn't realize I had been so neglectful in my Summer care. And here on the unchinked flag terrace are several clumps of asters, miniature wild ones. They, like the trees, found a foothold and sent down roots.

I must inspect the stone walls before the heavy frosts come. I must see that the walls of the house itself have no cracks where the Winter's moisture can creep in and freeze and heave those walls apart. I must look again at the timbers holding up the roof of the root cellar, see how persistently the carpenter ants have worked in them. I must patch the roof of the woodshed, snug the door of the pump house.

I own this land and everything upon it; or so says that piece of paper I call a deed. But frost and ants and vines and trees recognize no such ownership. It is mine only so long as I can hold it, keep the upper hand, maintain my little mastery.

FALL EQUINOX. Once more I have been telling myself that Fall is the most beautiful time of any year; and thus I know that all is well within me. I say that each Fall, and I mean it; and when April comes I say no other season can match Spring. That, I think, is as it should be, in my world, each season in turn labeled best of all.

Fall is a time of color and plenty and fireside peace—or such it should be in any well-ordered world, and thus it shall be when we have set our world to rights again. But it is also, to me, a time of gentle melancholy, mild enough to be a light mood and not a growling discontent with everything in sight. In its wake comes cold and bleakness, when stout walls and a warm roof are a human necessity. There is something of vanished youth in the sight of falling leaves; of equinoctial storms— which the meteorologists tell us are not equinoctial, but which come more often with the equinox than not; something of years as well as the year come to harvest. The wind eases over the hilltops, as though it came out of a distant past; or it roars through the oaks, impatient to be elsewhere. And thus my own thoughts, which are more emotion than thought, really. For this is a season of mood and memory.

Spring is the time when the urge to go seems strongest in the young heart; but now is the time when I would wander—now, when the sun is yellow as beech leaves and the moon the color of a sour gum against the night sky. The answer to my moody questions is there beyond the road's far turn or beyond that corn-shocked hilltop. Why there, I do not know; I simply know that there is where I must go. And I know, too, that from there I shall return, still seeking; for these questions have no answer. I cannot even put them into words. But each Autumn they hound me with a sweet, faint melancholy.

I T won't go down in the history books under that name, but this year might be called The Year of the Tomato. Is there a gardener in sight or hearing who hasn't all but buried himself under tomatoes? Of course not. They have even been harvesting tomatoes from city window boxes. And right now suburbanites in frost-haunted regions are rapidly burying themselves under green tomatoes while they frantically scald, crush and strain the last high tide of ripe ones and fill the new ketchup and chili sauce kettles.

An American Year

Nobody would say anything but the kindest words for the tomato. It is a friendly, healthful vegetable, or fruit—and let's not quibble about classification. It oozes vitamins and even more delectable things. It has flavor and substance and color. If it doesn't help you to see at night, it should, for it outsells carrots on most tables. And it certainly helps you to see on the morning after.

In any normal season there are just about enough tomatoes to go around, generously. Somebody sees to such things. But this season everybody with a spade blister on his hand set out tomato plants, and the season—in these parts anyway—was just right for tomato culture. We've been stuffed to the ears with them for two months, and now we've stuffed every jar in sight with them. We're about ready to call it quits. Until along about Thanksgiving time. By then we'll be back to our normal vitamin deficiency and ready to say from the heart, "And we are thankful, too, for all those jars of wonderful tomatoes—if they haven't spoiled."

FALL rain is full of weary leaves and September chill and the feeling of work done and changing season. It has the subtle smell of stubble fields and woodsmoke and Autumn plowing, and the feel of frost at hand. The roadside streams are littered with the castoff garb of a Summer gone, and the ponds are brown as the cattails on their marshy margins.

Fall rains come and settle down for a while, as though at one visitation to restore the whole of late Summer's sun-sucked moisture. There is a persistent generosity to an Autumn rain that breeds monotony, and

RAIN BY GEORGES SCHREIBER

then slow irritation, within me. The earth needs rain; but does it need so much without pause? When I have worn soggy shoes and a dripping raincoat three days in a row I begin to wonder if there isn't some means of distributing the weather, particularly the wet weather.

But there is no sense of malevolence in a Fall rain. It comes, and it continues, and a world whose Summer's work is done is cleansed and refreshed and made ready for Winter. This takes time—and rain. No

105

An American Year

Summer's country boy was ever quite cleansed, particularly if he has roamed the fields barefoot, in one quick scrubbing. Eventually the clouds will be rained out and the sun will be in sight again. The clouds are breaking now, in fact; I can see a long sun-shaft off there to the west. By tomorrow the world will all be bright, the skies clear as a youngster's eyes. And here will come crisp Autumn striding through the woods in a crimson shirt.

FIRST frost has walked through the valleys under the half-moon. I could hear it whispering through the fallen leaves as it hurried down the hillsides in the evening, feel its crisp breath as it passed me on the lower road. And at dawn I could see its path, glistening on the goldenrod stems and powdering the purple asters. Midmorning, and the tender gardens in the lowland had limp and blackened rows of tomato vines to mark its footsteps.

First frost is like a newcomer in a strange country, following the beaten paths of the valleys. It camps in the low meadows, gathering strength and biding its time. First it nips the grasses and the soft creeping plants. Then the bushes, where it curls the leaves and makes the spiderwebs a gleaming filigree of crystal. Sometimes it may even creep halfway up a swamp maple and then turn back uncertain of its grip.

Meanwhile, there will be mornings when the valleys are lakes of mist, with the frost there beneath them. There will be noons when the valley air is almost touched with June. There will be evenings when the long light on the hillsides is full of magic. And there will be nights when the woodsmoke wreathes the starlight in the hollows.

106

But once first frost has passed this way the pattern is set. It will come again on clear, still nights, and with each coming its path will lie higher up the Autumn hillsides. And at last it will walk the ridges, leave them, too, shimmering in the dawn. And after that the frost will walk boldly over the land.

REFLECTIONS OF GLOUCESTER BY JOSEPH MARGULIES

OCTOBER.

IT IS GOOD to live in a land of changing seasons. Particularly a land that knows Autumn. Not so much as a relief from Summer, but as a season in itself, an annual time of maturity, of mellow ripeness and rich fulfillment. Now comes the season when we know again the certainty of achievement, the calm surety of all that is meant by harvest. Now comes the time when day and night are in balance, when work and rest and dreams and reality have their proper places.

If we could know one year for what it is before we have known too many—years, one after another, merely as a sequence of time— we might reach earlier understanding. For the Fall of any year is more than three months bounded by an equinox and a solstice. It is a summing up without the finality of year's end. It is ripeness, not only of valley corn and hilltop bittersweet but of the mind and the understanding. It is a pause between growth and the long white sleep, when there is time to savor the sweetness of harvest, of crisp morning sunlight, of full-kerneled thought and sun-ripe emotion.

The sun is benevolent, and it is now true to the compass; it rises, for these few weeks, east, and it sets west. The moon has a horizon roundness and a zenith gleam that warms the wondering heart. The stars make their rounds without falter, but their paths somehow seem more clear in the Autumn skies. And thoughts follow a clearer orbit, now that the year's growth is at its summary and the instinctive reaching for the sun has become a root-strengthened communion with the earth. If there is ever to be understanding, surely Autumn will be its time. Autumn, with its clear-skied summing up and its long Summer yearnings brought to fruit.

THE sumac was the first to color, as always. Then the birches and a few of the maples turned, and the hickories. And after them the ashes and the sour gums. And now there is color in the oaks. The woods are lovely.

It is always a little startling to look off through the woods on a late September morning and see blue sky where only a few days before there was nothing but the green wall of leaves. There is the blue sky in the distance, marked off only by branches that have lost their foliage almost overnight. The whole world seems to have expanded. October can come pouring in.

Look up any valley and you can see it now. Or look to the hilltops, where tulip trees are shedding gold and sour gums glow with purple as well as red and orange. There is even color on the long-dead snag of lightning-blasted maple, for the woodbine has crept up its trunk.

And on the hillsides the dogwood greets October with bronzed leaves and lacquered berries, the spice bush gives its red fruit a golden setting and the viburnum turns crimson and purple. Or, if you would have even more fiery color, look to the brambly blackberry and the curiously tangled huckleberry bush.

There it is, the whole range of color, sparkling in the treetops and filtering down with the sunlight, the south-slanting October sunlight. Six months ago it was bud on the branch. Four months ago it was shade overhead, fresh and green. Another week or two and it will be a brown crispness underfoot. And there will be the horizon, the far horizon, for anyone to see.

T H E fruit of the barberry gleams in my Autumn woods, and I know it does not belong here. If anywhere, it belongs in town hedges—prickly hedges that scratch and tear the flesh of unwary passers-by. The birds probably are responsible for these plantings in the woods, possibly bringing the seeds from barberries that still cluster around an old home-site in the back pasture where some housewife cherished, and her farmer husband tolerated them long ago.

Its smooth leaf proves that it is no native. The American barberry has a leaf resembling the holly, and I should welcome it if it chose to grow here. That is sentiment, and nothing more. Its berries, too, are lacquer red and add a rich touch of color to the October woods; but when I think of barberry I think of golden yellow, the rich yellow of Navajo buckskin.

An American Year

It is the western barberry—called *Berberi fremontii* in the books—that I remember. To the Indians it was a dye plant. From its bark, particularly from the bark of the roots, they extracted a liquor that stained their dressed deer skins a color like the desert sun. They used it for other dying, but chiefly they used it for their soft garment leather, and anyone who has seen a Navajo in ceremonial finery must remember it.

In wheat country, of course, the barberry is a pariah plant. One particularly destructive variety of rust, which causes vast damage to cereal grains, passes its spore-forming cycle of life on the barberry leaf. So if you value a wheat farmer's friendship, never mention barberry without a properly bitter adjective. The gold in his vocabulary stands for fat grains of rustless wheat, not sun-yellow buckskin.

BEFORE the frost and gusty winds have thinned the leaves to a mere memory of their prime glory, take a look at the sassafras. A long look, for it is one of the grand trees of the woodland in any season, and particularly in the Fall. Its color? Name your choice, for you'll find it golden yellow and bronze and almost purple and, at times, a strange sassafras orange. It's a tree of pronounced individuality, even in dress.

There is no typical sassafras leaf, for instance. Some are simply eliptical. Some are shaped like mittens—and even there the sassafras refuses to conform, for those mitten leaves are both left- and right-handed. And some are doubly mittened, if you will, like an old-time farmer's work mitts, with a thumb for either side.

More than that, its branches follow no pattern, unless you call it a pattern when the limbs are complete individualists—some horizontal, some almost vertical, some twisting in absolute grotesquerie. And its roots are as vagrant as its branches.

But in one thing it is completely sassafras—its pungent flavor. Bite a fresh green twig and you have tasted a flavor never to be forgotten, a flavor that pervades root and branch and bud and leaf. Sassafras tea, that clear red-amber brew, is this essence distilled. And out in Indiana— perhaps elsewhere as well, but the Hoosiers are masters at this—they make a sugar-water beer which takes its substance from the sap of the maple and its flavor from the root of the sassafras. Its authority comes from the sunlight on a warm and yeasty keg. Describe it? Not even a Hoosier can, adequately. You simply sip it and glow. Glow like the sassafras tree glows in October, gold and bronze and purple and that strange and lovely sassafras orange.

OF THAT sugar-water beer which the Hoosiers make I have, to my regret, only a passing acquaintance. Its quality I know, and its temper. But how it is made was, until a few days ago, one of those state secrets which Hoosiers seemed reluctant or unable to communicate to an outsider. But at last one of the natives, properly primed, came forth with the following recipe:

"Take three barrels of sugar-water (maple sap to you) and boil it down to one. Pour in a crock or two of yeast, beat up, add a few cups of strong essence of sassafras roots, red and puckery and pungent. The barrel sits in the Autumn warmth for a few days, and inside something nice happens; bubbling with joy, the mixture almost laughs as part of the sugar is changed to alcohol. You should possess a big-bellied, clear glass pitcher to contain this grand, clear, pink, sassafrasflavored nectar. Cooled to frostiness, it makes glad yourself and an old crony or two. The maple and the sassafras have mingled their juices to a great purpose."

An American Year

HIGHLAND LOGGING BY DAVID STONE MARTIN

If I had three barrels of maple sap and a vat in which to boil them down to one, and if I knew how big is a crock, I should be tempted to experiment.

I AM no master with the ax, being a plainsman born. Oh, I can bring down a tree, if need be, and no one will mistake the job for that of a beaver with three teeth missing; and I can split an oak log with perhaps better than average facility. But my ax-work is in no sense artistic, and I know it.

But give me a two-man crosscut saw, with a partner on the other end who has a sense of rhythm in a strong right arm, and I can do a job. Not all day, perhaps, but for quite a few hours on end, if I have but periodic pauses in which to sit back and puff my pipe and survey the fruits of my labor.

There's something in the rhythm of a two-man saw that satisfies my soul. But that rhythm must be precisely right. Too fast, and there is no time for breathing. Too slow, and the saw hesitates, hangs its teeth, gets nowhere. And there is a proper touch to each stroke. You pull, and you press down just enough to get a bite, and you relax and ride back with your partner's pull. Or, if the saw is freshly sharpened and the wood of a proper texture, you press down not at all but let the saw carry its own weight through the log.

Two-man sawing can be a test of friendship as well as cooperation. The slightest twist on one handle at the proper time can freeze your partner's stroke; or you can wear him out by simply weighting your hand on the backstroke, thus forcing him to do the heavy cutting while you ride free. It can be a tricky business, as two mischievous boys I know particularly well can testify. But when they are in a tricky mood, I set them up as partners and sit and enjoy my smoke; and when they have pranked enough we get down to business again, and the sawdust flies.

THE Sky Walker will be abroad tonight. He always walks the moonlight, and tonight there will be a full moon. Autumn moonlight in particular, when the katydids have almost ceased their rasping chorus. No doubt the Sky Walker strides the land at other times, but I most strongly feel his presence when Autumn quiet lies upon the hills.

An American Year

Come out in the moonlight with me and watch the treetops, if you would know the Sky Walker. The night is silent as a moonbeam, the trees themselves untouched by so much as a wisp of breeze. Now there is a far-off whisper, a crisp sibilance in the distance. It grows, and the leaves of a whole treetop are in motion, crisp Autumn leaves not yet fallen from the branch. Now the next tree is touched, and the next, and a whole path of rustling leaves is becoming evident. Here comes the Sky Walker, striding through those treetops, scuffling the leaves ahead of him as a schoolboy scuffles the roadside leaves on his homeward path at sundown. Now he is overhead, and now he has passed us completely by, and there is silence again, the silence of still leaves in October moonlight.

I am sure that I have never seen the Sky Walker, and that I never shall. Sometimes he seems to be there in a wisp of mist; but at best I have seen nothing more than his mist-white moccasins—perhaps not even the moccasins, but only the momentary scuffle of mist risen dust-like from his footsteps. I have never seen him, but I know he is there, making his moonlit rounds when the leaves are brittle with Autumn. I have heard him often, as he passed by. Particularly when the moon is at the full and I myself am full of understanding.

THE name "Indian Summer" has no valid relationship to the Indians that I can discover. There was no such season on the Indian calendar, which reckoned time by the moon and not the weather. The moons were named for the weather or for the seasonal occupation, but I can find no Indian Summer moon.

There is a story I have often heard, and still disbelieve, which has it that the Indians waited for what we call Indian Summer as a signal to get in the last of their crops and snug their lodges against the coming blasts. It is a pleasant fiction with no particular basis of fact. Any countryman, white or Indian, uses the fine days of Autumn to finish off the season's work, so far as it is ever finished.

There is the story, too, that the early settlers gave the season its name because it was then that they saw the smoke from Indian fires as a blue haze against the distant hills. True, the Indians did set fires in Autumn, both by intent and otherwise, and the smoke hung in the calm air as a lovely haze, if it were far enough from the observer. But white men, too, set Autumn fires. And white men's fires made, and still make, Autumn smoke. To call it Indian Summer because of that smoke is to distinguish among arsonists and worshippers of bonfires.

What matter the name or its origin, anyway? Indian Summer, or White Man's Summer, or plain Autumn Interlude, it is grand, magnificent, thoroughly enjoyable. Bask in it, let it seep into your soul, and hope that it is not too soon ended.

WITH due caution I can now report that the last of the katydids seems to have been silenced and the stillness of Autumn is upon the countryside. The caution is advised by experience, for though the first stiff frost should put an end to the raucous katydid, it sometimes doesn't. The night-criers crawl away into cracks and crannies and emerge the first warm afternoon and stridulate their sluggish wings. But there hasn't been a sound from them for a couple of weeks now.

They were in full clamor, however, for at least ten weeks, which

An American Year

COUNTRY CROSSING BY CARLOS ANDRESON

should scotch that old belief in their ability to forecast frost. Year after year I hear somebody say, "First frost six weeks after the first katydid." And I begin to count the weeks, shivering in anticipation though I know there's no truth in it.

This year I made careful note, and if the superstition had been sound we should have been frosted shortly after Labor Day. We weren't, of course. And the katydids seldom come much closer to the first-frost date than they did this year. But I know that I can cite my

118

dates for years to come and still be told, firmly and decisively, that katydids are weather prophets. Thus do we cling to our favorite superstitions.

No matter. Now the Autumn silence is upon the countryside. The rumble of freight trains rolls across the night, but nature herself is retiring into the stillness that will deepen into December and icy January. The katydids were the last of the night-criers to go. Now the darkness belongs to the fire-tenders and the watchers of the stars.

THIS day I am thinking of a Navajo prayer-song, though I am far from the bright land which inspired it. It came to mind this afternoon as I returned from a walk through the woods and over to the hilltop where the ripe grass stands golden in the long light. This is the way I remember it:

> To the house of my family, there I return.
> Child of the yellow corn I am
> And to the Red Rock House I return.
> Where the blue kethawns are at the doorway, there I return,
> The pollen of evening light on my footsteps.
> At the yuni the haliotis shell hangs with the pollen,
> Twirling, going around, around.
> With it I return.
> To the house of old age, there I return;
> To the house of happiness, there I return.
> Beauty before me, I return.
> Beauty above me, I return.

An American Year

Beauty below me, I return.
Beauty all around me, with it I return.
Now in old age wandering, I return.
Now on the path of beauty I am.
There I return.

THE pumpkin is a melon, they say who would be scientific, a gourd-like herb of the family *Cucurbitaceae*—and any resemblance to cucumber in that name is not coincidental. The pumpkin vine creeps along the ground, an earthy plant, and puts forth blossoms beneath the notice of anyone less than a bee or a farmer. Its fruit is easily mistaken for a gourd, while it is still young and indecisive; but it grows and grows and grows, and at last it ripens to a glowing golden yellow. It is, indeed, the harvest moon of the Autumn fields.

The cucumber becomes a pickle. The gourd becomes a dipper, a birdhouse or a rattle with a staccato voice and name. But the pumpkin, if it is fortunate, becomes a pie.

It isn't that simple, of course. The pumpkin needs cooperation; and it needs a knowing hand as well as a generous heart. It must have eggs to give it life. It needs milk; better yet, thick cream. And salt and sugar. And those critical elements—the cinnamon, the nutmeg, the ginger, the cloves, the allspice. Finally, a crust to do it justice. Thus a pumpkin becomes a pie. Or does it?

Look at its color. Is there the glow of October in its open face? Its texture—is it creamy, yet able to stand on its own? Sniff its fragrance. Does it have the subtly blended aroma of the open fields and the spice shelf in the kitchen corner? Then taste it.

The fortunate pumpkin is a noble fruit, a joy in the mouth of mankind, a paean of Autumn on the happy palate. All it needs is a cook fit to be trusted with its potentialities. The unfortunate pumpkin, of course, becomes a jack-o'-lantern. Unhappily, there are cooks who still don't know the difference.

SYCAMORE balls hang pendant in the old giant down at the corner, and I have been trying without much success to trace the name "sycamore" back to some base of reason. The search leads me through Old French and Latin to the Greek "sykon moron," or black mulberry, a name originally applied to a native of Asia and Africa. The sycamore of the Bible is thought to have been the Egyptian sycamore of today, actually a fig tree. But in Europe the name is given to a maple tree. And here we know an American plane tree as the sycamore. The name has traveled far, both in time and space, and it has leaped, squirrellike, from tree to tree. I suspect that some crusty old Crusader took it back from the Holy Land and misapplied it in Europe, and that some early immigrant hung it on the wrong tree here.

But here it is, after a devious journey, and only occasionally do I hear it called by the more aptly picturesque name "buttonwood,"—a name which the old-timers used in recognition of the buttonlike fruit balls, which might in backwoods imagination have fastened the shaggy greatcoat of some legendary woods-wanderer.

It is not a tidy tree, by whatever name. It sloughs off the bark of its middle-aged branches in brittle slabs, leaving gray patches that gleam in the sun like splashes of frost or whitewash. Its Autumn leaves are an undistinguished rusty yellow. Its branching is random and scraggly. But it is a hardy tree and a welcome sight along the streams, where it sometimes grows to an astonishing girth. The veteran down at the corner is all of six feet through, and in the South its kinsmen grow even larger. It has no particular commercial value, but it played an unsung part in our history, for many of the ox-yokes that hauled the Conestoga wagons west were made of its wood. Not of sycamore wood, though; those yokes were fashioned from buttonwood.

OCTOBER sunlight, particularly morning sunlight, has a special golden warmth that adds a peculiar glow to life. Part of that glow, to be sure, comes from the earth itself, an October world with grass turned gold in ripeness and maples showing first color and sumac crimsoned with anticipation. But there is also a directness of the sun riding an east-west course, a simplicity of day begun at a proper hour, a pleasant air of Autumn.

If I face the morning sun anywhere in America I feel these things. On the East Coast it comes streaming in from the Atlantic, a sun that has warmed the mists of the fishing banks and is already touching the Allegheny heights with dawn's benediction. In the great Midlands it leaps the shadows of the eastern highland and pours its warmth down across the cornlands, themselves golden with the ripening husk and the wind-torn tassel. Muddy waters gleam and sparkle in willow-bordered eddies, and high bluffs glow red and yellow as the Indians saw them. An October day moves westward.

STEAMBOAT ROCK, WYOMING BY PHILIP CHENEY

I have watched the aspen glow of the high Rockies come to life with sunlight, and snow glittering on the high peaks; seen the sun move on to the high plateaus and the shadowed mesas where sage is gray and green and lavender and grass itself is bronze. On to the firs and larches that still clothe the western uplands, and the dark rivers with Indian names. And on, at last, to the live oaks and the brown hills and the shingle beaches of the Pacific.

123

An American Year

I can feel this October sunlight gathering color all across the land, east-west sunlight that has the glow of life, the subtle pulse of the year's own heartbeat.

A TREE in Autumn is a lovely sight. One tree alone can concentrate the beauty of a whole woodland, leaf by leaf and branch by branch, as one flower can give the essence of a whole garden. For the beauty of the turning woods is not alone in the scarlet of a maple grove or the sun-gold glow of a hillside stand of beeches. It is in the subtle change that creeps along the leaves themselves, from point to point and vein to vein. A woodland in full color is awesome as a forest fire, in magnitude at least; but a single tree is like a dancing tongue of flame to warm the heart.

Watch even a single branch outside a certain window, and you are watching the color of change. One morning there is a spot of yellow on a certain leaf, yellow which has not yet quite achieved the glow of gold. Another day and that glow may be here. It spreads. The spot becomes a splash of gold, edged perhaps with a thin line of scarlet. It creeps down the leaf between the veins, and then across the veins; and the scarlet edging widens into a band and then a border. And meantime other leaves have begun to turn, some to gold, some to dull bronze, some to blood-red beauty. All on the same branch, yet not two alike either in pattern or coloration. And finally it is a branch as full of color as the whole woodland.

Thus comes Autumn, leaf by leaf and tree by tree; thus the woods become a hooked rug flung across the hills with all its folds and all its colors as they came to hand. I can pause beneath one tree and look up and see Autumn on all the hills of America. I pick up one leaf of those already cast adrift and hold Autumn in my hand.

124

THE cricket is a small, black, ambulatory noise surrounded by a sentimental aura. On occasion it lives in the open fields, but its favorite habitat is behind the couch or under the bookcase in the room where somebody is trying to read. It has six legs, which make it an insect; two antennae, which make it a creature of sensitive feelings; two wings that can be scraped together, which make it a nuisance.

Only the male cricket scrapes its wings together to make the characteristic noise—or song, as some insist on calling it. The female has more important matters to attend to. Houses where people wish to read are chiefly inhabited by male crickets. E. H. Scudder, the entomologist, found out years ago that the common black cricket's notes are pitched in E natural, two octaves above middle C. Today, most of the crickets around here are flat. I have also found that their customary tempo is 80 to the minute, but they frequently skip half a beat, which is very upsetting to the listener. Perhaps these crickets have hearts which beat 80 to the minute and skip half-beats.

Few adult crickets are supposed to survive the Winter in this climate. But few adult crickets around here know when Winter begins. They start scratching wing on wing in August and keep it up until the wings wear out. Then they quit. Maybe they die. But their wings are discouragingly durable. And there's a new cricket crop each Spring.

In China they hold cricket fights for sport; or they did until more important fighting engulfed them. Such a custom has the particular virtue of eliminating one cricket in every fight. And the Chinese do not consider the "song" of a cricket cosy or sweet or even domestic. The Chinese are wise.

THANKSGIVING BY DORIS LEE

NOVEMBER. NOVEMBER

is cold rains and raw evenings and bright, crisp days and a few fugitive snatches of Indian Summer. It is brown oak leaves fluttering in the sunlight which slants from far to the south. It is blue jays screaming and juncos twittering and a swift, silent flight of teal beating downwind in the early dusk. It is crisp frost in the dawn.

November is a hearth fire and apple cider and pumpkin pie with plenty of spice in its brown goodness. It is topcoat and gloves and a muffler under the chin. It is storm doors and storm sash and an icy fringe along the streams. It is clam chowder and pea soup and chile and Irish stews, with lots of potatoes and onions in them.

An American·Year

November is rubbers and galoshes and umbrellas and sniffles. It is ashes from the furnace. It is a busy bucksaw, for the countryman. It is Election Day, orderly and democratic. It is Armistice Day, when we remember. It is Thanksgiving, when we are humble.

November, late evening of the year.

AUTUMN is a time of remembering. All the seasons of the year are compressed into the sere rustling underfoot; the frosted leaf is last Spring's bright treetop, last Summer's shade. But there are still longer memories on an Autumn hilltop, in the smell of woodsmoke, the rhythmic echo of an unseen axman, the yelp of a hound after a rabbit. And in other simple things as well.

The cidery scent of windfall apples lying in the midday sun. The raucous cry and flashing wing of a blue jay in the naked woodland. Two boys hulling black walnuts. A man in a windbreaker bolstering an old stone wall against the heaving frost. And a girl on a hilltop, a bunch of bittersweet berries in her hand.

Simple, obvious things. But there beneath the apple tree stands the shadow of Johnny Appleseed, primitive Christian and orchardist of the wilderness. The deep-stained fingers of the boys with the walnuts are a reminder of that America whose handmade woolens were dyed with the juice of those same native nuts. And stone walls—no matter where they're found—somehow echo New England's rocky hills, New England's Yankee twang and granite character.

Echoes and rememberings of a way of life, of folk and folkways

128

as native as corn bread and pumpkin pie, of a way of living that allows a man to own a hilltop and to look from it into a future of his own devising.

THERE are the fragrances of Autumn, too, the wisps of scents remembered and the faint, familiar odors. The winey smell of oak being cut to fireplace length by a ringing buzz saw. The sharp spice that lingers on the hand when a last, late chrysanthemum leaf is pluck-ed. The allspice-and-vinegar tang of a country kitchen with its final batch of sweet relish or pepperhash in the making. The tantalizing scent of herb bunches drying in the loft. The dusty sweetness of the hay barn. And the earthiness of a root cellar, with mingled odors of potatoes and turnips and onions.

They are the odors of good living—of an America with cordwood piled high, long ranks of preserves in the storeroom, full barrels and bins for the Winter's fare.

Yes, there are long memories on an Autumn hilltop. Memories of men who goaded ox teams over unmarked trails to the interior valleys in search of homes. Men who carved farms out of the forests with saw and ax and infinite patience. Men who set up courts and government in new towns and territories because it was their instinct to live a peaceful, orderly life. Men who built security for themselves and their families because they believed that thus could their whole society be made more secure.

Autumn echoes their dream, with its harvest and its tradition of thanks for the season's gathering. Summer has withered away, its heat as well as its foliage. Winter still lies ahead. The haze of Indian Summer softens the landscape, even charitably softens some of the memories. For the memories are not all sweet; they, too, have their allspice-and-vinegar tang. But they do add up to a way of life that is our own and that we still believe is good.

THE winds are shaking the acorns out of the oaks. They patter on the roof like a scurrying of small feet, and they litter the driveway. Next Spring they will be sprouting in windrows along the edge of the drive, and I shall be pulling them like weeds to maintain my mastery; if I let them go for a few years I shall have to hack my way through with a brush hook.

With memories of the sweet savor of mast-fed ham and bacon, I gathered a sampling of acorns one Autumn and tasted them, both raw and roasted; and for my curiosity I had an oak-tanned taste in my mouth which endured for several days. But acorns are edible, and some are sweet as chestnuts, notably those of the chestnut oaks. No chestnut oaks, however, grow here. Mine are black oaks and red oaks and white oaks and pin oaks, and their acorns are full of bitterness.

It was such bitter acorns, though, that provided food for Indians of the Pacific slope. They gathered them before they were ripe enough to fall of their own weight, shelled them, ground them in stone mortars and leached the bitterness away by pouring water over the meal in a coarse sieve. When they had finished they had a brown mass of dough which they boiled up in a kind of mush that tasted not unlike some of the cooked cereals that we are offered today—and that is no compliment to the taste of either.

Such acorn meal has been found to contain 5.7 per cent protein,

18.6 per cent fat, 65 per cent carbohydrates. What the remaining 11.3 per cent consists of, I do not know; but I have my suspicion. It is tannic acid, pure and undiluted. It is the undiscovered factor which persuaded the eastern Indians to grow maize though they lived in one of the world's largest forests of oak trees.

APPLES and potatoes are now stowed in the root cellar, and I have been gloating over the jars that stand in more or less orderly rows on the shelves. We shall struggle through the Winter somehow; of that I am now convinced.

Thinking thus, I am reminded of an uncle who, though he always lived close to the country, was haunted by the fear of starvation. Unless his wife "put up" five hundred quarts of fruits and vegetables each Summer, she was dooming him to a slow and painful death. Come September and he must have no less than three barrels of apples—preferably five—to stow away. Then came potatoes, at least fifteen bushels; onions, no less than three bushels; carrots, beets, turnips, parsnips—all by the bushel. And there must be a barrel of cider, a barrel of kraut, two kegs or more of pickles, half a dozen hams, flitches of bacon and side meat, stone jars of sausage.

He had a huge basement beneath his house and a capacious root cellar outside, and unless both were so full that he could barely wedge his way inside he spent all Thanksgiving Day groaning over the pangs of imminent starvation. I always thought he died in disappointment, for it was kidney trouble, not lack of nourishment, that finally did him in.

There may be a touch of his haunting instinct in me, but I doubt it. I am still the small boy who gloats over jams and jellies and gives the root bins and vegetable shelves only a perfunctory glance of satisfaction. It's good to know that the staples—the substance of a Winter's living—are there; but I could no more be content with those alone than I could with a house having no books, no pictures and no heart full of songs and laughter.

T H E sun sets early. The moon is late. Only the stars light the evening sky, the bright belt of Orion, the low-swinging Dipper. Familiar stars, stars with which I have lived since the Autumn nights of boyhood wonder years ago.

I watch those stars this night as I go to the woodshed and somehow feel a new kinship with them. I look to the north, toward the Pole Star and Casseopeia and Cepheus. I am a landsman, no seafarer, but those stars salt my blood with such spray as beaded the beards of Leif, called The Lucky, and his shipmates. I see those stars as the Vikings saw them, steered by them across the cold northern seas and came to Vineland, probing the mists of a strange unknown. I have followed those stars over many a far horizon.

I turn to the south. Andromeda rides high, and so does Pegasus. But the Southern Fish is low, and so is the Eagle, off to the west, low enough that I might have steered by them, roving the reefless reaches of the vast Pacific in my Polynesian proa when this America of mine was an unsuspected world beyond the sea-mist horizon. And I know that there beyond the dark horizon of this night are other stars. The Southern Cross, of course, which we never see up here but which I must have known in another age.

THE UPPER BAY, NEW YORK BY GORDON GRANT

Stars, a whole skyful of stars, and a November night, and a man with an armload of firewood. And race memories, the mystic kinship with men and places long ago and far away. But my stars, as it is my night, and my thoughts questing the night skies and the glinting stars of a past as nebulous as the frost of my own breath, as real as the fire-trailing meteor that whips across the dappled darkness.

133

An American Year

CONNOISSEURS of honey declare they can tell in one taste which field or tree its makers haunted. I am no expert in those distinctions, though I have never yet mistaken buckwheat honey for that which came from a clover patch. But I do know that there is a difference in jellies, even among those from a common species.

I learned long ago that there is wide variety in the fragrance of apple blossoms. Go to any flowering orchard and you will find a dozen different scents. The Winesap bloom has more spice in it than, say, the Rome Beauty or the Greening. And when the apples have ripened and the cider flows from the press, the tongue can note the same distinctions. Carry it another step forward, into the jelly glass, and still the difference holds. To draw a bold example, who can mistake the flavor of crab apple jelly? The difference is less perceptible, perhaps, but still there when one chooses among Winesaps and McIntoshes and Jonathans and Ben Davis's.

So, too, with grapes. There are wild grapes on my hillside, all superficially alike. But, even as with wine grapes, those in one situation get more sunlight or a different diet from the soil. And the jelly made from their juices reflects that difference. There is less difference between the patches of wild blackberry, but their jelly has a tang that no tame blackberry ever achieved.

When I try to describe the differences apparent to the eye, however, I am lost in a spectrum of translucent beauty. I hold each glass to the light and my eye can see the subtle variation in color, but how describe it? And why attempt? This is a beauty to be shared in the sunlight or at the dinner table, not on paper.

THE fall of Eden must have come at about this time of year, for where is the mortal who can turn his back on such orchard bounty as now invites his choice? Baldwin and Rome Beauty and McIntosh, Delicious, Winesap and Black Twig. Jonathan for the lucky, Greening for the patiently persistent.

But as I range the Autumn valleys jeweled with ripe apples and fragrant with the tang of cider, it is not the shade of Adam that hovers there above the orchards on the skyline. It is gangling, buckskinned Johnny Appleseed who seems to stride the ridges in the half-light of evening, the core of a half-eaten Northern Spy in one hand, a grin of pleasure on his weathered face.

More than a century ago Johnny Appleseed in the flesh was striding thus along the hogbacks. Chapman was his family name, though few cared or remembered, and he was Yankee born. But he early turned his back on salt water and headed west across New York State and down the inland rivers into the Ohio wilderness. His head was full of scriptures and his pack bulged with apple seeds which he planted wherever he found an open hillside. Countless trips he made, gathering seeds from the cider mills of New York and Pennsylvania, planting apple trees and the word of the God of Moses in virgin soil. And those who came after marveled at the beauty of Spring in his footsteps, the Autumn bounty that marked his path.

Eve was tempted and Adam ate, but Johnny Appleseed passed by and left his memory in ten thousand orchards.

A PROPERLY tended hearth fire warms my soul as much as it warms my body. Sometimes more. To be sure, not every fireplace is a joy and a comfort to the shivering heart. Too many builders never learned to construct a proper flue, and too many buyers never learned to look behind a fine colonial mantel. Moreover, even the best of fireplaces calls for a wise keeper of the flame—and the art of fire-tending is by no means a universal accomplishment.

Like all the arts, fire-tending calls for patience and tolerance. Patience with the simmering log and the slow flame. Kindling makes a quick heat and a flare of fire, but lasting warmth comes from the leisurely fire and the bed of embers. And there must be tolerance; of ashes, for one thing. The fireplace shoveled and swept clean each morning is doomed to failure; all it does is burn wood and burn it quickly. A hearth fire needs a bed of ashes, deep and comforting. The real fire-tender cherishes his ashes, gloats when they top the firedogs, beds his backlog in them and achieves a hearthglow that will outlast any blizzard.

The mantel is a facade, after all. The andirons are there only to keep the logs where they belong. It's the flue, the shape of the smoke chamber and the fire-tender's skill that makes a fireplace function. And the wood, of course. Best of all, wood that you've cut yourself; for, as the old men used to say, "He who cuts his own wood is twice warmed."

SOCIOLOGISTS, community planners and housing experts can cite impressively profound reasons for decentralizing industry and population, but not one of their arguments is as impressive as a clear November evening in what they call "the circumferential area." An evening with stars and a touch of frost in the air, with leaning birches and wind-stripped maples on the skyline, with lighted windows down the road and a dog barking someone welcome.

They are on the right track, but "optimum use" theories and "sociological factors" leap right over fundamentals that are so simple they are ignored. The crispness of a leaf drift underfoot; the soft outlines of a wooded ridge across the valley. The experts speak of "dwelling units," when people live in homes filled with family life; of "tenure" when every foot of ground and every timber and brick and stone have been possessed by human sweat and toil and love and tears and laughter.

The facts are there and the reasons given are sound, but the intangibles are missing. A youngster whistling on a hilltop. A boy and girl walking arm in arm beneath the stars. Talk and laughter heard momentarily through an open door. The reassurance that awaits a man when he can stand under a night sky on his own earth—earth that has felt the fang of ten thousand Winters and the healing touch of ten thousand Springs.

There may be centrifugal tendencies in concentrated populations, but there is also the kinship of man to the country.

THESE frosty days bring back memories of steam rising from the scalding barrel and butcher knives whetted razor-sharp, memories of hog-butchering time, when the Winter's supply of pork was prepared for the smoke house, pickling tub and sausage jar.

If the master of the job was a real old-timer, the scalding barrel's water was fortified with wood ashes instead of lye; but in any case the porker's bristles were loosened and scraped off with more vigor than ceremony. The carcass was quartered by the master hand, leaf lard stripped out and heaped in the rendering kettle, hams and side meat trimmed and prepared for their cure, more perishable delicacies set aside.

Then the feasting began. Fresh tenderloin was cut thin and fried to a turn. Pork steak, pork chops and side meat generously striped with lean were sizzled in the big iron skillet. While the sausage grinder turned and the fragrance of sage and black pepper tanged the air, spareribs simmered and pork roast browned in the oven. And when the lard kettle had done its duty, crisp golden cracklings were left to shorten pie crust and hot biscuits. Meanwhile, great pots of headcheese and scrapple simmered on the back of the stove, thickening for their molds.

That was hog-butchering time in the days that were. Beef-butchering was more specialized and fewer farmers engaged in it. But you could virtually smell your way from one farm to the next, sniffing the sausage and sidemeat fragrance, in rural America when the frost had come to stay. Hog-butchering time was as American as Thanksgiving, and almost as tasty.

WINESAPS make the best cider. Say it firmly and you may spare yourself some of the argument. Not all of it, but some. Better yet, set out a jug of Winesap that has been allowed to assert its character just the proper length of time, pour a brimming glass and hand it to your visitor. Then there will be no more argument between you for perhaps an hour—time enough to bare the bottom of the jug.

There are acceptable variations, of course. Blends, really. Ben Davis for body, Baldwin or McIntosh for an undertone, Delicious or Gilliflower for aroma, just a touch of Hyslop or Red Hibernian for tang, and Winesap for the dominating flavor—there's a blend worth a second sampling. Some dilute the Winesap with Jonathan or Northern Spy or York Imperial, with satisfactory result; but without one of these four dominating the whole, the mixture might as well be dosed with benzo-

THE GOLD TRAIN BY REGINALD NEAL

ate of soda and sent away to market. Cider should be had fresh from the press, the press of a man who has due respect for nature. In such a state it is the very essence of a peaceful Autumn, a drink as mild and soothing as fresh milk. Savor it then; but let your indulgence be only a sampling. Set it aside and give it its own way for a time, until it begins to stir with life and individuality. Now note how it tingles the palate and frolics on the tongue. Watch it closely, and sample it day by day. The time will come, if you but wait and watch, when at the first sip you will know that there is moonlight and fire-glow, frosty sky and shimmering sun. Let it go another week and there will be lightning in

139

a sultry sky as well. So make your choice—fire-glow or lightning; and restrain your thirst.

Into the apple go the rains of April, the blossoms of May, the sunlight of June, July's hot glow, the ripening of August, the maturity of September, and October's vigorous tang. From such a combination—naturally—can come an infinite variety of liquid phenomena. If handled with due respect and proper reverence this is one of the most delightful beverages native to the land. But you should start with Winesaps. . . . Here, have another glass!

TOMORROW there will be feasting and public prayer and thanksgiving, and some will remember that this custom rose out of the stony wilderness of New England when a handful of pilgrims thanked providence for life itself—for a roof, a fire, walls against the wind and the wild beast, for a few bushels of nubbin corn.

I walked under the stars this evening, and I saw Orion, the Hunter, rising out of the East, and when I came back up the hill I saw that Aquila, the Eagle, was there in the West, over our own land. As I walked I thought of those things for which I am thankful. Of this land, which was big enough to encompass a great dream and make it reality. Of mountains and mines and woodlands and rivers, of farms and ranchlands and towns and cities. Of the men of this land, and the women, of their individual dreams; of their machines, their factories, their skill and ingenuity.

But men die, dreams pass, machines molder away. And I was thankful for the sunrise of a new day, for sunset, for work well done, and for rest. For the fragrance of honeysuckle in June, pinewoods in December, for starlight, for the rainbow. For friendship, for the laughter of a child, for the love and understanding of a woman's heart. For the ideals which lift mankind out of bigotry; for freedom of the mind, of the spirit, and of aspirations; for adventure into far places of thought as well as far places of the universe.

I was thankful, too, that the grit of this land's soil was between my teeth, the fever of its swamps was in the blood my grandfathers gave me, the bruise of its stones was on my feet. These things, too, are a part of my heritage. And of all these things I was thinking as I came up the hill, facing Aquila, the Eagle, in the western sky.

STILL AS THE NIGHT BY S. L. MARGOLIES

DECEMBER. AUTUMN ENDS,

not by the calendar, but by the season itself. The leaves are gone, save those few parched hangers-on that will cling the Winter through to the twigs of oak and beech and ironwood. The weeds have ripened and their pods are empty. A few jays remain, and the earliest juncos are dropping in; but even they speak softly now.

The quiet days and the silent nights are at hand. One walks abroad in the hushful evening, a quiet so deep that footsteps are exaggerated even in their echo and voices carry on the chill air an amazing distance. So deep the silence that we shall hear the faintest whisper of the first snow.

An American Year

Gone is the crisp rustle of September leaves. Gone the loud complaint of the katydids, the crickets and all the other insects of early Fall. The frogs and peepers are silent. The chipmunks are resting from their frantic scurrying of the harvest season, and the squirrels go quietly about their business. Winds that rushed through the treetops of six weeks ago now sway the naked branches with a cold swish. Even the streams have ceased their brawling.

Winter creeps in, silent as the stars; only when it is full upon us will it howl around the house corner and rattle its icy knuckles at the door and windows. It is as though time itself were now at rest for a moment, a solemn pause before the season of the Nativity and the turning of the year.

LOOK UP, these December evenings, and there overhead you can see the constellation known as Pegasus. Particularly you can see those four bright stars which form the Great Square of Pegasus, one of the major constellations of our universe. To the east, halfway to the horizon in midevening, is a lesser group known as Taurus, the Bull; and off to the west, close to the horizon itself, is Aquila, the Eagle. But when you lift your eyes, there is the Great Square.

As with all the major constellations, there is a legend that goes with the Great Square of Pegasus. It is the story of Medusa, the very embodiment of terror and horrible fate, who lived near the realm of the dead and who could turn a human being to stone with one glance. Medusa was feared and hated even by the other gods. But finally Perseus rose and, in the strength of righteousness, not only slew but beheaded her. And from the blood of slain Medusa sprang Pegasus,

144

the winged horse of hope and dreams and poetic truth. In due time Pegasus was immortalized in the heavens, his four bright stars forming a huge quadrilateral for all to see.

In the astronomers' tables, and in the tables of those who ride the skies and know the stars as friendly and unswerving guides, the four stars of the Great Square are sometimes known by number, sometimes by letter, sometimes by the names Markab and Scheat and Alpheratz and Algenib. Whatever the names, there they are, an enduring foursome on which travelers may fix their course, a group representing hope and winged dreams and truth, which sprang from the death of terror.

T H E leaves lie deep in the woodland and the slanting sun lights the floor of the deepest thickets; the rest that is Winter seems to have come over my acres. But when I go out now I see the humbler greenery of this world, the venerable ancestors of those bigboled oaks and broad-topped elms and white-barked limber birches. Now the mosses and the creeping pine and cedar and the hardy ferns have sunlight to themselves.

In green Summer they are lost to the eye. You feel the deep mats of tree moss underfoot in the shade where the meadow meets the woods, but you see the grass. The teeming colonies of hair moss and broom moss are there at the gnarly butts of the swamp maples, but the violets catch the eye. And the ground cedar is lost in the green shadows of the underbrush.

Now I see them plainly, unexpected green gleaming through the rifted leaves. The persistent fronds of the Christmas fern spread their grace against the gray stones of the old wall. The grape fern, beginning

145

to turn purplish bronze, thrusts up through the dead grass. And the tangles where shadows once lay so deep are now alive with the green runners and spreading heads of running pine and all the other Winter greens that are known as club mosses.

They are old and humble and patient dwellers of this earth. Their kind are found in fossil beds, so like those we have today that there is no mistaking them. They were here long before the oaks and the maples, yes, and the violets and buttercups. It is good, and it is healthily humbling, to see them now, when the long, cold days stretch ahead. All things come, in due course, to their season in the sun; and this is theirs, literally as well as figuratively.

WHEN I look out the south window and see the sun staring me in the face, it's Winter, and no use going to the thermometer or the calendar to prove the sun is wrong. It certainly isn't Fall, even though custom insists that the solstice which doesn't arrive until late next week marks Winter's official entrance. Fall is pretty well finished, in this latitude, by the end of November.

As a matter of fact, the equinoxes and the solstices are arbitrary limits set by those who were more interested in quartering the year than in facing the reality of weather. Maybe a little more sunburn and chilblain and a little less eyestrain over astronomical tables would have provided a better calendar of the seasons. Why, after all, do we have to say, "Well, Spring is here," in the midst of late March's sleety rain, and tuck our muffler tighter about our quinsied throat? And why can't we be honestly grumpy the last week in November and say, "Yeah, the Winter has already got my joints to creaking," instead of shrugging it

SILENT SENTINELS BY S. L. MARGOLIES

off with a bright, "Brisk Autumn day, isn't it?" chattered out through teeth that are clicking like refrigerated castanets?

Well, there's the sun, streaming directly in through my south window. And taking such a short-cut toward the southwestern horizon that it will put in a scant nine-hour day when its year-round contract calls for twelve. Yes, it will be working overtime next July, but who wants

An American Year

more sun in July? Build up the fire. Put on a sweater. And recall that a year ago today the temperature sidled down to 6 below zero in this district. Oh, yes, the official temperature was only zero. But officially it was still Autumn, too.

SNOW belongs to the countryman. In the city there is little beauty or wonder in any snow that falls, except as it is seen sifting down in a dappled curtain that whitens the rooftops and window ledges. In the city's canyons it becomes slush and ice, a darkening nuisance to be plowed aside and carted away.

But in the country, where it can lie as it falls, white and new and softly heaped, snow is full of loveliness. If it is a wet snow it clings to trunk and branches, accenting the clean, simple line that only nature can contrive. In the meadows it softens the stark outlines of leafless Autumn, and in the lowlands it decks the bushes and fringes the dark pools.

There is magic in any snow, for it gives the whole scene a new setting. But there is a particular magic in the first snow of the Winter, for eyes that have not yet forgotten Summer's green lushness and the bright display of Autumn can see it whole. A little later the freshness will be gone. Snow will no longer be clean and new. The Winter world will even seem a little drab without it, drab and Winter-bleak.

But the first snowy morning in the country is filled with wonder and the realization that snow belongs to the open fields and rolling hills, to the peaceful land of homes and hearthsides and fertile acres.

THE confirmed early riser has a fine scorn for the sluggard who chooses to breakfast in the sun. Such a one misses the best part of the

148

day, says the dawn-worshipper; which is so many words through a hat, for the best part of any day is the chooser's choice. But the time is now upon us when even the sluggard can face the dawn at a civilized hour —the sun itself isn't up until a bit after seven. It's a good occasion to see what the virtuous shouting is all about.

Frankly, it's about chilly rooms and cold water in the hot-water faucet, a sluggish heating system and an outdoor temperature down in the twenties. It's about a world so quiet that the quinsied crow of a shivering rooster half a mile away echoes all down the valley. It's about air so brisk it tweaks the nose and shocks the lungs into quick defensive action.

But it's also about a world that has been jeweled in frost. Grass crackles underfoot as a million tiny crystals are crushed. Weed stems are fringed with miniature ice gems. Twigs are decked in finery that is the envy and despair of jewelry designers. The lingering leaves of the wild strawberry are outlined in gleaming crystal fringes. A stray spider-web is a net of frost-pearls. And if one will but visit a still, small pond in such a dawn one will find a tracery of ice so delicate it would seem a human breath might shatter all its exquisite beauty.

There is no denying that any dawn is a lovely thing to watch—from a well-warmed bed. But if one must meet it face to face, this is an excellent season for such a sacrifice. Spring also has its points, but the April dawn comes shortly after midnight. Or so they say.

FROST deepens in the earth and primal forces gather strength as Winter tightens its hold upon the land. Now comes the time when the very mists shall rend the rocks apart. The feathery snow shall gouge

149

An American Year

WINTER IN THE CATSKILLS BY DORIS LEE

new valleys in the hills and the adamantine mountains yield to the subtle strength of their own cloud wreaths.

Who can devise so simple a lever as an ice crystal? A drop of water lies limpid on a great rock. It rolls into a hollow, finds a crevice not even the thinnest root could penetrate, and it creeps in, a faint film of moisture. The cold comes. Ice forms. And the rock is heaved in twain. Man does it with a driven drill of steel and a blast of dynamite. Nature does it with a few wisps of mist from the clouds of sunset.

Walk in the boggy edge of a meadow on a Winter morning and

the whole crust of the land crackles and crumbles beneath your feet. It has been lifted from its subsoil on a million tiny needles of ice, lifted and stirred and opened to the air. Man does it with a sharp-shared plow. Nature does it with the seep of an Autumn drizzle.

Ice in the rivers. Ice gnawing at the shores of the ponds. Ice heaving the cornfields with their ragged stubble. Ice loosening the rocks in their beds and scarring the shoulders of the stubborn hills. Ice, older than the continents, as new as the latest frost.

Armies march and dictators rant, and ice on a river turns the flow of a battle. And long after the dictators have been laid in the frost-heaved earth a wisp of cloud and a crystal of ice will be moving the granite mountains.

C O L D, like virtue, is relative. Its severity depends on where you are and in what circumstances. Statistically it depends on who takes the temperature readings and where. That accounts for the Weather Bureau's insistence that it is 9.8 degrees above zero, or 8.9 perhaps, when the countryman knows by observation as well as experience that it is below zero.

Weather men, of course, are conservative even when they are free to discuss the weather. When the countryman speaks of a mean temperature he means mean, cantankerous, downright cold, ornery and uncomfortable. But to the weather man a mean temperature is just average. That is typical of their divergent viewpoints.

The countryman reads his temperatures from the thermometer out on the front porch. The weather man takes his data from a sheltered thermometer. The countryman lives with his weather; the weather man puts his weather down in the record books. So when the official thermometers stick at 9.8 above zero—or is it 8.9?—and the unofficial thermometers show zero or 8.9 below, you have a working example of relativity. Not the Einstein variety, but a kind that the fellow with frost-bitten ears can understand if not wholly appreciate.

That, by the way, may explain some of those old-fashioned Winters. Their records were kept in many instances by men who lived with the weather. The temperatures were down-to-earth. Compare them with the front-porch observations of today and you may find that grandfather wasn't so badly abused by the weather after all. He simply faced the facts as he saw them right there on the front porch.

THE WIND, breath of the passing year, keens through the treetops and moans in the chimney's throat, and in the Winter sky it sends the low clouds scudding. It is a snow wind, an ice wind, a wind that bows the birches and creaks the oaks and strips the last few shriveled leaves from the beech and the ironwood. A mountain wind come down, wolflike, to course the valleys of the world.

Panes quiver in their sashes and the fire leaps on the hearth, and there is no sound above the wind's rush. Not only through these trees, not only down this valley and over this hilltop, but far across the dark horizon. Somewhere out there it is wallowing a deep-laden ship and smothering it in icy spume. In some far night sky it is drowning out the drone of an air liner's motors, beating on great wings driving through the darkness. It is lashing bitter rain like sleet into the face of a lone herdsman shepherding his flock homeward across some lonely mesa. It rattles cold knuckles at some door where a long life nears its

December

WIND-SWEPT PALMETTOES BY W. R. LOCKE

end, and it echoes the first cry of a life newly begun in some remote cabin where love has made life good.

Wind that sent men questing all around the globe, in their cockle-shell galleons. Wind that drove them up the river valleys from the ocean, and through the woodlands and across the prairies. Wind that keeps the dunes forever shifting. And the dunes are like the longings of mankind.

The whistling wind of the year's end, unseen, not to be grasped and held and braided like a cord, but to be listened to and understood like an ancient and unending rune. The cry of days past, the call of days to be.

WINTER arrived this morning, by astronomical calculation. If you care to look it up, you can find the exact moment when the sun reached that point in the ecliptic at which it attains the greatest southern declination. In other words, we have come to the Winter solstice.

Even for those who have to live with it, Winter is a remarkable season. Year after year it comes adorned with snowflakes, ice, poinsettias, colds, narcissuses and last year's overcoats. It affords the farmer time to finish last Summer's work and to contemplate next Summer's job. It keeps the urbanite in touch with the principles of combustion and radiation. It enables Florida to sell sunshine and New England to sell snow. It brings long leisurely evenings in which to read digests of books one would enjoy reading. Winter is wonderful.

Not the least of its wonders are the phenomena of time, temperature and transition. The cold, which has been merely fumbling around, now will settle down to business. But the daylight, which has been steadily wasting away, will get a new grip on life. Nights will be colder, but shorter. And somewhere up ahead lies that day when a lasting thaw will set in and the buds will put forth leaves.

No Winter ever was all skiing or sitting by the fireside, and this one will be no exception. There are no such exceptions. It will have its rough, tough days. It's Winter, isn't it? But there have been just as many Springs as Winters, in the affairs of men as well as of meteorology—and you needn't trouble to look *that* up.

THERE was a fine, dry snow last night, about six inches of it, and the day's cold—it was down to zero, except in the full sun—made it good for skiing. Good for my kind of skiing, that is; I speak not for either the professionals or for those young daredevils who think skiing is 99.7 per cent flying down an interminable mountainside carefully studded with trees, rocks, stumps and sundry barriers, natural and artificial. Mine is a more primitive type of skiing. I merely go places and come back, without benefit of cable tows.

So this afternoon we got down the skis from the loft and went places. We went through the woods, into the old orchard, up the hill with all the birch brush and over to the far pasture. If you are a ski-run skier, as I understand the matter, you do not go through the woods except on a path laid out by a landscape architect carefully brought up on a diet of icicles and arnica. But we went through the woods very much the same as we go through them in Summer or Fall, taking a bearing and going there, through or over or around intervening thickets and bull briar tangles. It calls for what I consider skill; certainly I am rather puffed up with pride when I have maneuvered my skis successfully through a brush patch that would halt a deer.

In the pasture we ran down a couple of hills, not for the running, particularly, but because we wished to get to the bottom. And eventually we came home again, having climbed four stone walls and gone through three wire fences. It was good skiing.

I like to watch the daredevils, and the flight of a master from a ski jump is wondrously beautiful. But I doubt that they get more fun from their skiing than I from mine.

OTHERS may think of the waning year in their own terms, but the countryman recognizes any year for what it is—another round of the seasons, another time of planting, of growing, of reaping. These are matters of eternal consequence, and nothing that man may do can change them. Not even his greatest folly—war—can blight for long the upward thrust of a seed, the lovely branching of a tree. And, mighty as man may be, he still orders his life by the sun, the tides and the seasons.

Toss in whatever records of the past twelvemonth you will, and when the totting is done there remains the fact that our land is still fertile, our crops have been bountiful, our rivers still flow and our mountains still stand in majestic strength. Take away all other possessions, and we still have those. And they add up to a mighty source of strength for any stricken heart. Man has but to step forth onto the enduring earth and lift his eyes to the everlasting skies to share in them. They are our inalienable inheritance.

Man has been living with this earth and watching the unchanging march of the seasons for hundreds of thousands of years. Periodically, the Goths, the Huns, the Vandals, the pillagers and ravagers, have swept across the continents in cyclones of violence and devastation;

and for a time it has seemed that the seasons were of less consequence than the sear of man-made flame and the scorch of human hate. But Huns and Vandals pass and their roads of conquest are lost in the furrows of time; and always there are warm Spring rains and blackbirds in the marshland and the Great Dipper swung there in the night skies. And men with freedom in their hearts to live with them and know the truth of time.

DEEP WINTER BY ERNEST FIENE

JANUARY.

A YEAR passes and a new year begins, and neither sun nor moon alters its cycle by a tenth of a second. Time runs out, we say. Yet water flows beneath the ice and winds sweep down the valley. The earth turns as it has turned for aeons on its axis.

Time is an endless cord in which man has tied many knots, that he may count them as they slip between his fingers. A life is time, the span between birth and death. There is the time of growth, the interval between planting and harvest. And there is the time of the mountains, which rose from the waters when the world was young. Knots on an endless cord.

One man boasted that time was his and that the next thousand years were in his hands. And for the passage of a few knots in the cord he seemed to speak the truth. Then time itself ran against him, and he could not stay the knots, try as he might. His was an old and empty boast; for while man may count the knots and call them his, no man can hold them long. A few knots in an endless cord, and the cord itself is time.

An interval has passed, a year, a cycle of the sun. We look back and gauge its meaning; and now we look ahead, fingering the knot, knowing how many days lie ahead before we can feel the next knot but having no knowledge of what those days will bring. And ahead, farther than any eye can see, stretch the years, time until the mountains shall be worn away and new mountains shall arise. But we do know that the water shall flow, even beneath the ice, and that man shall look to the stars, and that freedom shall be his to defend as long as the knotted cord shall flow between his sentient fingers.

WHATEVER else you choose to say about January, it does bring days that are lengthening instead of diminishing. The sun will be in the sky today about ten minutes longer than it was a week ago today, and the span will steadily increase until next June. One of these fine days, indeed, it will even be possible to eat a reasonably late breakfast without benefit of artificial light.

The farmer, of course, is used to getting up in what city folk consider the dead of night. Some farmers take a zestful pride in doing the morning chores, eating breakfast and starting a Winter day's work by lantern light. Only the sluggard lies abed until a reluctant sun creeps over the horizon. All of which perhaps induces a superior sense of satisfaction. But I suspect that it depends upon the man. I do know that no sensible rooster lifts his blear-eyed head to crow dawn at five o'clock on a January morning; and I know, too, that I should pot any rooster that showed any such tendency on my premises. Further, it seems to me I am betraying my human heritage if I allow a barnyard fowl to dictate my day's beginning—or its end either, for that matter. Am I a man, or am I an outsize Minorca rooster?

Of all the year's seasons, Winter is the time when I most appreciate the sun. True, it's a cold and distant sun, impersonal as an icicle, at this time of year. But it gives me the illusion of warmth, even now, and of the eternity of my cosmos. I do my best work by sunlight—or at least I do good work more easily. That is one reason for welcoming January. It brings more snow, more ice, more cold, but it also brings more sunlight. It got its name from Janus, who specialized in new beginnings. He was a two-faced fellow, of course, but that was only a personal eccentricity. One of his faces was rather nice. So is one of January's.

WINTER has its compensations. Soup, for one. What can surpass the leisurely delight of a steaming bowl of full-bodied soup after a brisk day in the open? Not as an appetizer. Not as a prelude to a meal. Simply as a meal in itself. With coffee, perhaps, or with tea. With crackers, if they are crisp and salty. But basically soup.

Pea soup, perhaps, full of substance and simplicity. Or bean soup, with the flavor of onion and ham bone. Or potato soup, also with onion and with crisp little cubes of salt pork done to a turn. These are the soups of my boyhood, and I shall forever revere the split green pea, the small white navy bean and the large speckled pinto bean, and the potato and salt-pork combination. In later years I added the lentil, a delight my boyhood never knew.

And there's clam chowder, for coastwise folk—and pick your own recipe, but give me the kind without thickening. Pepper pot, for Pennsylvanians and other fortunate folk. Plain vegetable soup, with everything from carrots to tomatoes, onions to peas—but no parsnips, please. For Midwesterners and those who have been there, chicken soup with homemade noodles, a Sunday dish that makes an occasion of any day in the week.

Beef soup, provided it is something more than meat juice and water. Mock turtle, if the cook knows her business. Mulligatawny, if it is the real thing. And take your pick of the cream soups, which are matters of taste and judgment, not to say inspiration.

There's a sampling, a beginning. America is rich with native soups. The important thing is to have a simmering pot of any one of them at hand when wanted, and a capacious bowl to set before the eater. Sing of Omar's jug and loaf if you will; I'll take the soup pot and bowl any Winter day.

O N E blistering day in June I expressed the wish to be in Bismarck, North Dakota, where the temperature was 43 while we here were sweltering in a humid 89. Well, you can have Bismarck now; I'll take Tucson, Arizona.

Oh, yes, the temperature got down to 35 in Tucson a few days ago;

COMPANIONS BY ALFRED RUDOLPH

163

but that was in the dead of night, when any sensible person would be in bed and under blankets anyway. And in midday it was up around 60—official temperature—which means about 75 on the sunny side of the square. And there's lots of sun in Tucson, a fact to remember in midsummer and to rejoice over now.

It was warmer in Tampa last week, and in Miami and in San Diego; but we stick to Tucson. Too much warmth in midwinter is as bad as not enough. In Tucson we could enjoy an evening fire on a fine old Spanish hearth, perhaps with the fragrance of cedar. And we could look off to the northeast and see the Santa Catalinas like cardboard mountains in the starlight, and know that there, not twenty miles away, the mercury must be playing tag with zero.

Yes, I'll take Tucson, which probably was visited by the Spaniards from Mexico in 1540, some eighty years before the Pilgrims landed at Plymouth or the Dutch at New Amsterdam. It's a good place to be in January. The natives like it in July, too; but that's another matter. I'll take it now. I would, that is, if I were there.

A LIGHT snow fell last night, and this morning we found deer tracks just back of the house. From their size, we guessed that a big buck, a fair-sized doe and a last Spring's fawn had visited us. Following their trail, we found that they had come from the north, through the old orchard. While they were here they inspected the garden patch and the compost heap and sampled the browse among the birches. Then they went up the hill and across the stone wall.

There was satisfaction in knowing that they came leisurely and took their time about going away. After they crossed the wall they went on up the slope, through the tall grass that stands like western bluestem, and on over into the blueberry patch. There they browsed for quite a while, long enough for the fawn to lie down and take a nap. Then they went into the thick woods, following a trail that many generations of deer must have used, so well defined it is. We turned back there, content.

It is good to know that they came to visit us and found no cause for alarm. They will probably come again. Now and then we see the white flash of some buck's hurrying rump when we go to the blueberry patch in Springtime or into the deep woods in Summer. There is plenty of cover for them, and these eastern deer require only a few hospitable acres. Once they have found a patch of woods and underbrush not too much frequented by men or dogs, they settle down and live there content.

It is not thus with the big mule deer of the West, which need wide ranges and travel far. But deer, like people, partake of the country. There are no wide ranges here.

GO OUT in a snowstorm clad in a dark coat and you can have a whole museum full of snow crystals to study simply by standing and watching the flakes as they fall on your sleeve. The variety is literally endless, but until you have tried to pair off the crystals it is hard to believe that a hexagon can have such variations.

Occasionally one will find a double hexagon—actually a twelve-sided crystal—but I have never seen one of these rarities which did not have six rays of one type, all alike, with six alternating rays of another kind, also all alike. It is as though two crystals had been superimposed

An American Year

in such a manner that the points of one came precisely between the points of the other.

Now and then, too, one will find a flake that is the simplest kind of hexagon, merely a plate with six square, unadorned edges. But usually the flake is a star, elaborate in the extreme, filigree work of amazing beauty. I have seen some that were half an inch across, large enough that one could study each point in detail; and the complexity

166

of each point was like the dream design of some master in balanced detail. But never did the points of a flake vary from each other; for there is a crystalline order in nature that is as near perfection as anything we know.

Watching these flakes upon my sleeve, so fragile that a puff of breath can destroy them, I thought of that other common hexagonal crystal, one of the most durable of all in the rocks of the hills and the sands of the seashore—quartz. There is, surely, some close cosmic kinship between them.

JANUARY is the depth of Winter, by custom and record, but as I walk through the frozen woodland even now I can see Spring on the branches and in the frozen earth beneath my feet.

The dogwood trees are laden with buds that remind me of a praying mantis' head. This year there is a wealth of bud on the dogwood, which should bring a flood of bloom, come May. The high branches of the maples—swamp maples in particular—are visibly tufted with tight little buds that will become a red haze in the treetops when the sun has climbed back from the south. And if you could reach them, as the gray squirrels can, you would find that the upper boughs of the black oaks are rough with buds. They aren't as big as those on the maples; but the oaks take their time about everything. The squirrels seem to find them just about right for winter fare.

Closer at hand are the spice bushes, with their tightly furled buds which have been there since the leaves first turned yellow in the Fall. These, too, are flower buds and will become a mist of yellow in the days to come, pinhead blossoms full of sharp fragrance. And if I look closely in the bogland I can find the green horns of skunk cabbage thrusting through the ice. Some say that skunk cabbage first shows green in February, some in March; but here it is in January, stubbornly defying those who would set any timetable limits on it.

It's January, all right; but January passes and April comes, always and forever. And those things rooted in the good earth make few mistakes. Before the leaf, comes the bud; and no bud is grown overnight.

WE WERE sawing firewood today and when we went to work on an oak log the saw bit into it with unusual ease. The reason was that the temperature was down below zero and had been there for several days. The oak log was frozen. Its tough fibers had become brittle. And when we set log sections on end and swung an ax on them with the force necessary to split them in, say, October, we fairly jerked our arms out. Those frozen billets popped apart with an almost gentle blow. Again, it was the result of the cold; they were frozen, and the freezing set up tensions that readily forced the wood apart with the relatively light persuasion of an ax.

Trees freeze, of course, in Winter, and they survive it with little or no damage if they are native to frosty regions. The place they would be damaged is in the cambium layer, the tissue between the bark and the wood which is the medium of a tree's growth. On its inner side the cambium produces the xylem or wood cells, through which water rises from the roots. On its outer or bark side the cambium produces *phloem* cells, through which manufactured materials are conducted downward from the leaves. During the growing season the cells of these layers are fat little masses of protoplasm with a semi-fluid consistency. They are

168

full of liquid, at that season. But when Autumn comes the liquid seeps out of the cells, by osmosis, into the spaces between the cells. Dehydrated cells are left like loose bags of gluey substance. When zero weather comes and the moisture freezes and expands, the cell walls are not ruptured.

That, roughly, is the explanation of a hardy tree's ability to withstand the cold. It freezes, as our oak log froze, and when billets of that oak were put on the fire they oozed and hissed with steam as any midsummer log might ooze. The water is still there. But the cells have achieved a flexibility, a natural protection, which spares them from damage.

CURIOUS about the fate of buds in this bitter weather, we cut a branch of dogwood, brought it into the house and sliced one of the big buds with a razor blade. Then we put the slice under a glass before it had time to thaw and could make out the minute crystals of ice between the layers of leaf and petal. It was frozen all the way through. But the freezing would not be fatal. Such buds would have opened quite normally next May.

It is when the buds have been deceived into untimely activity that the damage is done by frost. We could not see, with our low-powered glass, how the moisture in the nascent leaves was distributed between the cells, but that is what happens here as well as in the cambium layer of the trunk. When Spring comes, however, or when February brings a deceptive hot spell, that moisture will be reabsorbed by the cells and growth will begin. Should a cold spell follow and deep frost sweep again through the woodland, the moisture will freeze again; but this time it will be inside the cells rather than between them, and the expansion of the ice crystals will rupture the cell walls. Then there will be damage. If the fruit buds have begun their Spring activity, that will be the end of this year's fruit crop. It is not the cold alone that does the damage; it is the unseasonal warmth followed by the cold.

These frozen dogwood buds were quite unharmed, although the very bark on their twigs was frozen tightly to the wood beneath. They were prepared for frost when it came, even for the deep frost that has lain upon the land for three weeks of unaccustomed cold.

THE meteorologists draw fine distinctions between snow pellets and sleet. In their business, no doubt such distinctions are necessary. They also distinguish between sleet and freezing rain. But when I am out afoot in a snowstorm and what have been soft flakes turn to pellets which are flung into my face with the force of bird shot, I growl at the "sleet" and let it go at that; my concern is to find shelter, not the exact word. And when I am abroad in a car and the precipitation turns from flakes to something which covers my windshield with ice and the road with a glare on which my tires can find no traction, I have no compunctions about snorting at "sleet" once more.

The meteorologist is thinking about what happened in the strata of air above the earth, which layers were what temperature and which ones were saturated with moisture. He is noting that snow formed at a certain altitude, that it started to fall as flakes, that it came through an air layer saturated with moisture still in liquid form despite a temperature well below freezing. That moisture, he tells himself, caught at the flakes and froze there, and since this layer of moist air

WINTER EVENING BY ERNEST FIENE

was deep, the original flakes emerged from it as snow pellets—such milky granules of ice as stung my face unmercifully when driven by this earth-wind. I call it sleet. The meteorologist reaches for a more distinctive word and comes up with the German term, "graupel." The only satisfaction I get from such a word is that it somehow reminds me of "gravel."

So I can tell myself that I have not been out in a sleet storm; I have been in a "gravel" storm. Look at my raw and ice-battered face and you might well believe it.

171

An American Year

I'VE JUST been growing the finest garden in the world, with a huge crop of tomatoes, cabbages, beans, sweet corn—everything that strikes my fancy. And flowers—the most magnificent flowers that ever bloomed! Right here in the easy chair beside the fireplace, I've been gardening; the chair with the stack of new seed catalogues heaped on the floor beside it.

It's a wonderful way to garden, really. The seed is always the best, always sprouts, never is frosted. The seedlings shoot up, strong and healthy, in the twinkling of an eye or the crackling of an ember. Are they tender? There is the patent cold frame, perfect in function and construction and set up before you could say "chrysanthemum." Exactly the right fertilizer is always at hand, in the proper combinations and in endless quantity.

And there are no stumps in this garden, no stones, no spots of acid soil, no reluctant clay. No trees with blighting shade. No gullies. Nor are there any slugs or cutworms or bean beetles or aphids or rose beetles. And there isn't a blight in the book that can't be wiped out by simply turning to page 67. And, glory be, no weeds!

What if it is January? What if the temperature is where it is? What if the snow is *that* deep outside? I'm gardening. And if May and June can bring one-tenth the satisfaction that glows in these catalogues, I'll be jubilant. Think of it: a garden like this, without one blister or one back ache!

THESE are days, and nights, for reading. New books, yes; but old books too. Particularly books about our beginnings and our growing up. And among such books I prefer those about people; the letters, journals, memoirs set down by those who lived through the early years and the troubled years; such times as the 1780's, the young 1800's, the 1860's. And records kept by farm folk and the little people of this land, as it is fashionable to call them; letters written by those who waited at home through the long years, by those who went forth to the new lands of the West.

Formal histories are all right for the broad story. That is a part of our heritage and education. We know the big movements, the political chronicle, the outlines of our national crises. But too often we forget, if we ever knew, how everyday life was lived in those days.

I want to know about the mother who wove her own sheets, ground her own meal, even plowed and reaped while her husband was off fighting the campaigns of New Jersey. About the boy of ten who had to be the man of the house and somehow manage the farm while his father went to Vincennes. About the family that started to Oregon and bogged down on the Platte, and made a home there. About the bride who went with her husband in an oxcart into the Ohio Country.

We have too few such stories in print, and of those available too few are read. It is there that we find the real history of America and its people, not in books ground out by historians steeped primarily in the writings of all the historians before them.

OZARK SNOW BY CHARLES BANKS WILSON

FEBRUARY.

FEBRUARY IS a monument to man's fumbling efforts to gear his life with the stars. It is also a monument to vanity, but that came a bit later.

When Julius Caesar came to power the Roman world used a calendar of twelve lunar months of twenty-nine days each, the remaining days of the solar year being parceled out whenever the priests or governors saw fit. But Caesar had an orderly mind and he called in Sosigines to draw up an orderly calendar. Why not, Caesar asked, divide the year into twelve months alternately thirty and thirty-one days long? Because, said Sosigines, that required 366 days, and there were only 365½ days, or approximately that, available. But in the new calendar Sosigines did accept Caesar's idea for every fourth year, and to make things come out right he clipped one day from February in each of the intervening three years.

This calendar of Sosigines—for which Caesar, as was the custom, received the credit—was so practical, so great an improvement over what had gone before, that it continued unchanged into the reign of Augustus. Then came the moment of vanity.

Augustus, too, wished to leave his mark on time. Caesar's name was commemorated in the seventh month. Augustus gave his name to the eighth month, grasping at immortality. But August was one day shorter than July, which would never do. So Augustus made them of equal length, appropriating the extra day from February, and his vanity was satisfied.

I think of Augustus—and none too kindly, either—each time I run through the old rhyme of the months or count on my knuckles to assure myself that October has thirty-one days and that April has only thirty.

O N E doesn't have to believe in groundhog day to believe in wood-chucks. There's a woodchuck burrow beside the stone wall above the old orchard, and since it is safely remote from the garden I am glad it is there. *Arctomys monax* is a good citizen, in my book of record. To be sure, I've never had a congregation of woodchucks resident in a cornfield, nor have those doughty old boys which tunnel under garden walls and leave a path of ruin and devastation behind them ever come my way. I can understand the feud that stands between victims of such conduct and all woodchucks; but I am no participant in that feud.

To me the woodchuck is a self-respecting old codger who likes his solitude, his leisure, his food and his sleep. When he has to work —as in excavating a new den—he works at high pressure and for long hours. Once the job is done, he relaxes and stays relaxed until the next need arises for concentrated effort. He is no high-strung busybody, and he keeps his nose pretty well out of his neighbors' affairs. He does not bay the moon or greet the sunrise with unseemly clamor.

He fattens in the Fall, when provender is plentiful. About the time of first frost he retreats into a den which he has prepared with appropriate comforts, and there he sleeps. Winter is a long nap, to him. I think he misses a good deal by hibernating, but he is entitled to his habits, which in this case disturb no one. He awakens in February, sometimes, but usually late in the month. And he enjoys the Spring and Summer as much as you or I, maybe more. He usually sleeps right through ground-hog day, which is another item in his favor; for more often than not it is a day to be passed by with a minimum of notice.

THERE is ice in the wheel tracks in the fields and on the footprints in the paths through the woods, thin, papery ice of the kind that forms quickly and then remains when the water beneath has seeped away. It crackles underfoot with a glassy sound, and when you look closely at a sheet of it you see that it has designs. The upper surface is smooth as a windowpane, but it is as opaque as frosted glass. Turn it over, and you see that it is, literally, frosted.

I looked closely at such a sheet today and found on its under surface as beautiful a pattern of ice crystals as I have ever seen. There they were, arrayed in swirls and feathers of the kind that frost creates on a damp room's windowpane. But these were not the thin, frosty patterns. They were made up of crystals as much as an eighth of an inch in diameter—solid hexagonal water crystals that looked for all the world like big grains of sugar, or of crushed rock salt such as we used long ago to pack the ice-cream freezer. But hexagonal without exception, the six-sided form in which water crystallizes, either in ice or snowflake.

There they were, those thousands of crystals, arranged in the patterns which shone through from the upper surface. In places they were piled half an inch deep. I could distinguish individual lines of crystals, and parallel lines of them, and layers of them along those lines. The curves might have been laid out with some intricate drafting instrument, so true their symmetry. The straight lines would match a ruler's edge.

Looking down on those ice films, I could see only vague patterns somewhere within them. But when I came down to their level and looked beneath I discovered a whole new world of beauty, something that matches a snowflake in perfection.

FEBRUARY can bring downright cantankerous weather. Bone-chilling cold has swooped down on us with a wind that bows the oaks. The mercury did not even pause at zero on its way down, and it is still falling. There was no sunset. The sky darkened throughout the afternoon and steadily lowered, and when it lay on the treetops the wind blew night upon us.

Thick walls are a comfort and there is a domestic cheer in the glow of the backlog in the hearth's deep ashes. On such a night as this it is easy to understand why home, family and clan were so important in the civilizations which rose in the northern latitudes. There may be happiness and understanding in a nomad's tent, and under a benevolent sun, but there is solid strength in a house of logs or stone that must stand up to the bitter winds of long nights.

I have set bricks on the hearth tonight, that we may carry some of the fire's warmth to bed with us. We shall wrap each brick in a newspaper and a towel and tuck it where the feet can find it; and I shall remember blizzardy nights of long ago. Grandmother did that, and so did Mother, before hot-water bottles came into fashion. A brick has scant comfort for an aching stomach and it refuses to conform to the contours of a throbbing head, but it has a great deal to offer a pair of wintery feet. Its warmth there at the foot of the bed sends its reflections all the way to the pillow.

The temperature still falls and the wind still roars, but there is snugness here and comfort and companionship. The night draws us all closer together. Surely it was not by chance alone that hearth and heart came so near to being the same word.

THE conquest of fire was one of the great achievements of man. I sit here and watch the glow of a log, the slow flame curling upward, and I am seeing in the embers many centuries of forgotten history. There must have been four stages in this story, four long and misty chapters.

At first, fire was a natural phenomenon, to be feared and perhaps

STEEL VALLEY BY LOUIS LOZOWICK

appeased. Lightning was fire, and there was fire in volcanoes. Man, like the animals around him, fled from such fire to save his life. But, being man, he pondered on it, learned about it. And thus came the second stage, when man took fire for himself and fed it and tamed it for his own protection. His animal enemies still feared it, and thus fire gave man a strength he otherwise lacked. His fists were no match for horns and claws, but the fire he could hold as a torch made him master of even the mastodon. It made reasonably safe his home, whether it was a cave or a cairn, and he could settle down in one place.

The next step is to me the most fascinating of all. Man learned to

180

make fire at will. He struck two stones together and made a spark. He twirled one stick on another and created a coal. That was the first great discovery, the primal invention. That was the turning point in human history, for without the means of creating fire man might have gone the way of the brontosaurus. Instead, he looked into the flames of his own making and saw the future there. Out of those flames came whatever of civilization man has thus far achieved. And that was the fourth stage, the use of fire.

My verb is wrong. That *is* the fourth stage. We are still learning how best to use our fires. Otherwise I should not be sitting here tonight wondering how civilized we really are.

LAST year we had a bird feeding station on a window ledge outside the dining room, but the field mice found it, climbed the wall and made it their major source of supply. So this year we hung that feeder on long wires from the broad eaves above, putting it a foot and a half above the sill and a foot out from the window. That ended the mouse forays. But now a gray squirrel has found it.

He is not a big squirrel; I judge him to be one of last Spring's babies. But he is wise and resourceful. He cares little for the grain in the feeder, but he has a great liking for the slab of fat ham rind we put there in lieu of suet. How he knew it was there, I do not know; perhaps he smelled it.

The first day he came he surveyed the feeder from the terrace, eyeing every angle and approach. It was swaying gently in the wind, and that obviously puzzled him. But he climbed the wall to the window ledge, sat on his haunches and waited. When the feeder swung

An American Year

WINTER MORNING BY ERNEST FIENE

close, he reached for the perch along one side, caught it with one fore-paw, was carried off the ledge and swung there like a boy on a trapeze. But he could not haul himself up and finally he let go. Up he came again to the ledge, and again he watched the feeder's slow swing. This time he gauged it precisely, leaped, caught the perch with both fore-paws and went up and in. And he came out with the slab of ham rind, leaped to the terrace and made his meal there.

The next day he was even more skillful. This morning he was in the feeder almost before I saw him on the terrace. And this morning he took the ham rind up a tree and stowed it in a crotch. I can't retrieve it there, but the birds can. And if young Grayback wants more he can have it. It's worth a slice of ham rind to see his sleek grace going through those acrobatics.

THE cold wave has vanished almost as swiftly as it came. It was down below zero last night, and this morning it is almost 30 above. So swift a change would never come in January; but this is February, and March is just over the hill. Only in a rare year could the bitter cold maintain itself now for more than a few days. And this is not one of those rare seasons.

The change, so swift has it been, reminds me of the coming of the chinook on the western plains. I have seen a February blizzard there heap two feet of snow on the buffalo-grass flats and send the temperature down to 20 below zero. In the days of open range, the cattle would by then have approached the end of their Winter's strength. In December they could stand up to such a storm and weather it nicely; but after a month or six weeks of pawing through the snow crust for their forage they were Winter-thin and Winter-weary. A week of that snow would mean heavy losses.

I have seen the blizzard end in midafternoon and the night clamp down like an ice sheath. Dawn fairly crackled with a temperature still well below zero. And then, before the sun was midmorning high, the chinook would creep in. Temperatures would fairly leap—as much as 20 degrees in an hour. By midafternoon there would be grass in sight where the snow had blown thin as it fell. By night, water would be flowing down the hillsides and eating the drifts away from underneath.

The chinook is a warm wind which creeps over the mountains and sweeps down onto the plains in late Winter. Some call it the snow-eater. We have no chinooks in this area, but the change that came in the night was fully as welcome as a chinook would have been.

FOR nearly two years I spent three hours each Monday morning on a high and windy tower on a high and windy ridge, watching for airplanes. Since the hours were 3:00 to 6:00 A.M., I saw a thousandfold more stars than airplanes. I saw Winter come and go, from there, and I heard the voice of the wind in many moods.

I listened also to the voices of a variety of men, for my companions on the watch came and went with the necessities of their own lives. It is a peculiarity of man that he often opens his heart, if not his soul, under cover of darkness; and when that happens a man reveals more of himself than he knows. But in that lonely time and place each one, without exception, fell silent eventually, realizing that his words were as nothing against the wind and his ego of even less consequence among the stars.

I venture that no one can face the sky and the dim horizon of night for hours on end and fail to catch somewhere in his emotional tinder at least one spark of humility. Seamen have it, and you can often see the deep glow of it in their eyes, particularly if they have been long away. Plainsmen have it. And airplane pilots who have had only the stars for companions on many nights have it deep within them.

Little men are almost painfully silenced by it. Their egos, like small pebbles, must have the resounding walls of a tin can to rattle around in; they need the reassurance of their own echoes. But there are also those in whom such humility engenders pride and exaltation. I shall long remember the February morning when a young scientist pointed to the stars of the Great Dipper and said, "We can plot their courses and analyze their spectra, but, thank God, we still don't know where they came from! Man needs a few enduring mysteries in his universe."

THE lichens on the stones in the wall outside my window fascinate me, not only for what they are but for what they mean—and I wish I knew more about them, though nobody knows all their secrets. This I do know, however: the lichen is made of two separate plants, a fungus and an alga. Neither could live on those stones alone, but by working together they thrive not only on these stones but on the rocks of mountains where no other vegetation can exist.

The alga needs moisture for its growth. It cannot manufacture or otherwise provide that moisture by itself. The fungus needs food which it, likewise, cannot obtain alone. But together, in an association known as symbiosis, the two of them can provide all the food and moisture either of them needs. Thus they grow, where nothing else can exist—no other form of plant life—the fungus capturing the moisture and the alga manufacturing the food.

Together they invade situations which would otherwise be doomed to eternal barrenness. And as they complete their cycle of life they leave behind them the beginnings of soil in which other plants may eventually take root. Even in lichens, however, there is a succession of forms. In the most exposed and unpromising places one finds the encrusting type, the kind that appears to be little more than a gray or bluish-green stain on the rocks. Give it slightly more favorable surroundings, and a leafy species appears. Enrich the environment a bit more and a shrubby species takes over, the kind best exemplified by reindeer moss. Give it really favorable conditions and such luxuriant growth as that of the Spanish moss develops.

But in all these species there is symbiosis, cooperative growth of a fungus and an alga. I sometimes wonder if the economists of this world mightn't study the humble lichen with profit.

IN ALL conscience, February is no time to think of haying; but I caught a whiff of haymow fragrance in an old barn today that took me back to a July bottomland where a clattering mower laid long swaths of belly-high bluestem. The sweetness of drying hay filled my nostrils and I could see my grandfather building a stack that would stand firm in the strongest wind, dry in the heaviest rain.

I could hear the rattle of hubs on axles as the hayrack moved down the windrows, and I could feel the ache of my shoulders in late afternoon after pitching hay since early morning—pitching it onto that rack in the field, pitching it off at the barnyard. And I could feel the sting of gnats, the bite of chaff under my sweaty shirt—though it was scarcely a nibble compared with the torture of barley beards in the harvest field. I could taste the half-warm sweetness of jugwater and feel its trickle down my chin.

But most of all I smelled the new hay, hay that had lain in the sun

BOY WITH COWS BY JOHN COSTIGAN

and cured and filled the whole valley with its fragrance. Not the
sweetness of alfalfa or clover or even of timothy, that rarity among
plants which bears a man's first name, not his last—it was named for
Timothy Hansen. The sweetness I best remember is that of wild hay,
which has more of earth and sunlight and Summer rain and less of
honey in it.

An American Year

No barn whose mow has ever been filled with hay ever loses that fragrance completely. Nor does any memory which reaches back to a Summer hayfield. No, not even in February.

THERE'S a new sound in the wind as February draws to a close, a new feeling in it. Not Spring yet, nor even the March wind we think of; but no longer the sleety blast of Winter nor the cry of the bitter gale at the doorway. This is the wind of change, the gusty breath of days with earlier sunrise, later sunset, warmer afternoons.

Crows call with a new note, still harsh but not quite so rasping. Blue jays look blue again instead of midwinter gray. Chipmunks are out and foraging. Push the soggy leaves aside and you can find green sprouts on the false strawberry, the cinquefoil. In well-sheltered spots there is the cautious upthrust of lily fingers, exploring the strengthened sunlight. Things are getting ready to happen, down there in the cold, dark earth.

The ice needles that had heaved the swamp muck are nearly all gone; you can walk there now without a crunching underfoot, on sleezy top-slush which hardens overnight. And in the meadows where the earth had heaved high around the rocks which thrust only a nubbin into the daylight, the soil has begun to settle back where it belongs. In the strawberry bed, too, where the mulch lies thin the soil is settling and the plants will have to be firmed back into place. There's much to be done in the garden, but February and early March are no time to do it.

Three more weeks and the Spring equinox will be here. Spring itself will be within hailing distance, and the peepers will begin to shrill. Bees will be on the wing. But now the winds of late February are blowing and there is still a touch of Winter in the air, at sunset if not at noon. Change is in the wind, the slow change of the deliberate earth.

FIGHTING MOOSE BY OTTO WACKERNAGEL

MARCH. THERE'S SOMETHING

about a March rain—even if it starts out as sleet or ends as short-lived snow—that partakes of the changing season. It isn't a warm rain, such as falls in mid-April. But it isn't the cold rain of November, either, cheerless and filled with Winter's warning. It's simply a March rain that cuts channels in the frosty earth and runs roily in the little streams, soaks into the open woodland and drips from the eaves without a trace of an icicle.

No weather man's Winter was ever ended or even cut short by a March rain, but the Winter of a weary soul can be lifted overnight by an evening's downpour. It changes the whole world, subtly, almost imperceptibly. One must seek out visual change, by lifting a dead leaf, by thrusting into the silt; but there it is, an eager sprout reaching for the sun, a spear of green thrust hopefully upward. The blind, however, could sense the subtler change. It is in the very air of the fields, an odor of life and growing things where only so short a while ago there was the smell of dead grass and moldering leaves.

Winter is not yet past. There is still ice on the ponds. There may be more snow, and there will be nights of biting frost. But there has been March rain, and there will be still more of it. April lies ahead, and May. It takes no communiqué to tell me that, for I heard the rain on the roof in the darkness of the night.

WE HAVE a family of young gray squirrels just across the way. The parents built a nest of twigs and leaves in a high crotch of the tall white oak that stands opposite the dining room window, and this morning the youngsters—four of them—were out inspecting the world. They're about the size of small chipmunks, and their tails are bristly, not yet long and full and graceful; but their color is the soft, silvery gray of all their kind.

The mother squirrel sat on a limb and watched while they climbed uncertainly about the big branches, never getting more than five or six feet from the nest. If it wasn't their first trip out, it couldn't have been more than their second or third, for the fear of the unknown was obviously upon them. The most venturesome of the four finally reached the next crotch above that which holds the nest, but there his courage gave out. He clung—desperately, it seemed—to the rough bark and whimpered, his small tail stiff and straight as a bottle brush. The mother coaxed and scolded, but he wouldn't move. Then she ordered him, peremptorily; and he backed down the branch, fairly quivering with uncertainty until he could dive into the safety of the nest; humiliated, perhaps, but out of danger. None of them stayed out more than ten minutes.

Some say that gray squirrels seek out hollow trees and never build twig nests unless the woods are crowded, but I can see a dozen nests from my front door—perhaps half of them in use now—and mine are not crowded woods. All those nests are in oaks or swamp maples, all forty feet or more from the ground. The material in the biggest of them would fill a bushel basket. I've watched those nests each Spring I've been here, but this is the first time I've seen the youngsters out and learning their way around.

IF YOU would hear the voice of the changing year, listen to a brook. The brooks are singing now, a sweet prelude to Spring. From all the hillsides where the snow lay deep the waters are trickling and whispering toward the valleys where they join the rising chorus of the brooks.

Spring comes first beside such waters. Grass begins to green in the moist lowlands, where flowing water has carried away the frost. Buds are fattest in the underbrush which has its roots in the brook's bank and which weaves its basketry of stems there in the brook's warm breath. The arums and the water plantains come first to life where the mist of a spring brook lies most persistent. The earliest of the violets will be found in the muck where brook waters rise.

There is still frost in the ground, and there will be ice over the ponds and ice to clog the brooks; but the waters are singing now as they have not sung in many months. And those of us who were Winter-bound for

193

weeks watch and listen to the flowing waters with perhaps too much eagerness. We are impatient for Spring. That is the way of the human heart.

But here is reviving life, live waters seeping from the earth and singing in the valleys. You can hear the song even from the hilltops, if you listen closely—waters leaping from stone to stone, rushing eagerly toward the rivers and oceans. And on a brisk morning you can see the mist of those waters curling down the valley like phantom streams. And you know deep within you that the cold residue of Winter is flowing out of the hills, down the valleys and away. You know that the brook's song is a song of vernal triumph.

I OFTEN wonder who built these stone walls of mine. I should like to thank him, or his memory. But nobody around here can recall him, not even the oldest inhabitant. He was a farmer, I'm sure, for they are such walls as farmers used to build to mark off their fields, laying up new stones each season as they cleared the ground ahead of the plow. But he is long gone, for any farming that was done on these acres must have been done before the big trees sprouted; and there are oaks here that lift their crowns seventy feet above the soil.

The builder is gone and forgotten, but I should like to thank his memory. As walls, his patient handiwork is not and perhaps never was a model of craftsmanship. The stones are run-of-the-field, poorly chinked and laid at random. But the walls testify to his industry, his honesty and his foursquare method of work.

The wall at the back of my land runs from the brook at the foot of the hill due west over the hilltop to the big blueberry patch. When the

COVERED BRIDGE BY ASA CHEFFETZ

property line was surveyed it did not deviate two feet from the wall at any point. The other wall bisects my land and meets the back wall in a right angle that is as true as any carpenter's square. And I can stand on this wall on a Winter's night, when the trees are naked in the starlight, and sight down its length and see the Pole Star there at the far end, high overhead. Perhaps he laid it out one Winter night himself. Certainly he knew which way lay north, and true north at that.

IT IS good to live with a wall that has its directions straight. We set our house facing the wall that runs north—true north—and square with it. Some of the stones that had fallen from the wall went into the foundation, and more of them went into the big chimney. But none of them came inside the house. They are outdoor stones which have dwelt with the weather and shaped this land. Any house built here should conform to that fact.

I say those stones shaped this land, and I mean it literally. The wall is a clear line of demarcation between boggy woodlot and upland slope. Below the wall are seep springs that flow briefly when the year is young, and deep black muck and swamp maples and black ash. Beneath the trees is a maze of spice bush; and beneath the spice bush are cranesbill and swamp violets and trout lilies and skunk cabbage and masses of ferns.

Above the wall is another land. It lies literally above the wall, too, five or six feet above the wood lot. And that is further proof that he who built my walls has long been at rest beneath his own stone, for the difference in land level represents the silt of decades that would whiten the beards of a father and his son. Here where the silt is deep are white oaks and tulip poplars, and up the hillside a bit are red maples and pin oaks and black ash, and still farther up the slopes are gray birches. There is no muck here, no violets, no skunk cabbage; wild strawberry takes their place, and sweet Mayflower and spotted wintergreen and humble ground cedar.

Once, I am sure, that stone wall simply marked the bounds of a field. But over the years it became a barrier which changed the land and its inhabitants. Perhaps there is a moral in that stone wall, if one were to draw long parallels.

THE wall is a world of small life, teeming and endless. Lift a stone from its bed of woodbine roots and leafmold and you will open a whole community of frenzied ants or scurrying beetles. Crickets chirp away their lives within its crevices. Spiders spread their nets across its crannies. Wasps house there. Butterflies at midday and moths at evening, monarchs and gypsies and swallowtails and skippers, rest on its stones. Toads squat in its moist shade and fill their palpitant bellies.

But when I look at the stones themselves I am looking at cosmic forces and the long, long history of this land. There was a time when I might have trickled this red sandstone through my fingers, in the days of the world's youth. Mountains have risen and been worn away and submerged in the oceans since that time. Mountains sat on the back of this granite boulder, and it once felt the fiery breath of the inner earth. This perfect egg of a stone was shaped thus in the swirling grind of a glacial pothole. This shard of flint tucked in a chink may have been discarded by an arrow-maker forgotten before Henry Hudson sailed up the river a few miles from here.

This sandstone, this granite, this shard of flint, were once the soil in which roots sought life for the leaves above them. They are stone now, and we think of them as unyielding and eternal. But they will be soil again, in another million years. Change is the only certainty, even in stones.

When I become impatient with the ways of man, I come here and walk beside this wall; and I thank the man who laid it up, the man who could look into the night sky and see the Pole Star eternally pointing north.

O U R baby squirrels were down on the ground today, for the first time. After that initial venture from the nest, they came out each morning, gaining confidence by the minute. The third day they were down at

An American Year

the second fork below the nest, and from there they could scurry up the tree almost as swiftly as their mother. But even on the fourth day they still descended the tree tail downward, in the manner of a black bear cub.

This morning they came on down the trunk. One of them pioneered the way and the others followed; but still they came down tailfirst, pausing often and complaining—or perhaps only encouraging themselves—from time to time. Five feet from the ground, the leader paused and waited for the one nearest above him to catch up. Then the two of them, side by side, descended to the big rock at the tree's base. They sniffed the rock—a new element in their lives—and their tails stiffened. They leaped to the tree and scurried upward two feet or so. Then the leader turned about and for the first time trusted himself to come down headforemost. He made it safely, paused for a moment on the rock, then tumbled off. When he picked himself up he ran perhaps ten feet on the open ground. But that was enough. He looked around, startled as a fawn, and scurried like a little gray streak. He reached the rock in three leaps, pounced from there to the tree and went up the gray bark all the way to the nest at top speed. The others caught his fright as he went past, and in two breaths there wasn't a squirrel in sight, big or little.

From now on they'll be coming and going many times a day. The mystery is broken. They have found the ground. The world is theirs— for a time. Boys head for the horizon, when they leave home, but squirrels head for the earth beneath their trees.

THIS is the time of year when I can readily understand sun worship. It's a pleasant sun, these March days; a benevolent sun which reaches into the east windows in the morning and into the west windows in the afternoon, and no longer sulks across the southern sky. It is not yet a burning sun; it is still coaxing life to come out and enjoy it. It is a sun to bask in, with an overcoat where you can lay your hand on it. It is a sun to walk in, through the still leafless woods where it can reach clear to the ground.

Even the March wind is tempered by this sun; and its warmth lingers faintly to take the bitter chill off the night. The night itself is not so long, now that the sun has swung back toward the zenith. It has broken the spell of darkness, as those who put their faith in the sun long ago well knew.

There is still ice on the ponds, frost in the earth. But the ice is going, and the frost as well; they have lost their grip as the sun strengthened. And life is stirring at the roots; sap begins to rise to the sun's bidding. Cut a spicebush branch, place it in a sunny window for a week, and you will have buds bursting, tiny yellow blossoms open to the sun. Rake away the deep leaves on a south-sloping tulip bed and you may find the over-eager shoot reaching for the sun.

Science can cite any number of facts about the sun; but in March I simply feel it, soak up its warmth, begin to glow with its benevolence. It is a good sun to have around. I can almost go pagan and bow down to it, on a warm March day.

TOMORROW brings another equinox, another Spring by the celestial calendar; and as I walked through the woods this afternoon and over onto the ridge I was thinking of Spring in Colorado, on the plains and in the high country; Spring in New Mexico and Texas and Carolina and Pennsylvania; Spring in the city and Spring here on these wooded acres. Chiefly, though, I thought of Spring on the plains; for this is the season when we are most aware of our beginnings.

An American Year

I stood on a hilltop and looked out at a world bounded only by a vague horizon; I lay on my back in the prairie grass and stared at a sky with no limits at all, a sky where only the great white clouds and the soaring eagle drifted past. A boy was of no consequence in that setting, but it mattered little. I could ride north to the sand hills and watch the breeze play on tall golden grass and see how the swirling wind carved huge, crumbling craters in the sand. I could ride south onto the hard flats and lie on my belly and watch prairie dogs and burrowing owls in their contentious rounds of life. Bullbats cried in the dusk, meadowlarks filled the dawn with song, and sunrise covered the sky with magnificence. Mine was a world without limits, a vastness full of wonders. But the eternity of wind and sun and rain and grass on the enduring hills was graven deep into my understanding. . . . Spring on the plains.

Those plains are far away and that time is long ago, as we count time. The west wind today was blowing from those plains, however, whispering in the leafless pin oaks on my hillside. It will be blowing long after I have gone from here. And the grass will green in April—here as well as there—and eagles will soar in a depthless sky. For these things endure—the wind, the rain, the sun, the green leaf and the spreading blossom; and men trying to live with them, fighting them sometimes, less often trying to understand, leaning a bit with the wind, facing the wind and the rain and the seasons. These things endure. . . . Another equinox, another Spring.